Mathias Lair
A la Fortune du Pot (Potluck)

THE TABLE BECKONS

THE TABLE

BECKONS

◆ ◆ ◆

Thoughts and Recipes from

the Kitchen of

ALAIN SENDERENS

Illustrations by Izhar Cohen

TRANSLATED AND ADAPTED BY MICHAEL KRONDL

FARRAR, STRAUS AND GIROUX

NEW YORK

Translation copyright © 1993 by Farrar, Straus and Giroux
All rights reserved
Originally published in French under the title *Figues sans barbarie et
autres propos de tables et recettes de Alain Senderens*, copyright © 1991
by Éditions Robert Laffont, S.A., *l'Express*, Paris
Published simultaneously in Canada by HarperCollins*CanadaLtd*
Printed in the United States of America
Designed by Debbie Glasserman
First edition, 1993

Library of Congress Cataloging-in-Publication Data
Senderens, Alain.
[Figues sans barbarie et autres propos de tables et recettes. English]
The table beckons : thoughts and recipes from the kitchen of
Alain Senderens / illustrated by Izhar Cohen ; translated and
adapted by Michael Krondl. — 1st ed.
        p.   cm.
Translation of: Figues sans barbarie et autres propos de tables et recettes.
1. Cookery—Miscellanea.   2. Cookery, French—Miscellanea.
I. Title.
TX652.S4613   1993   641.5—dc20   93-15912 CIP

CONTENTS

RECIPES

BY CATEGORY

INTRODUCTION
THE FIVE SENSES

◆ ◆ ◆

A native of southwestern France,
Alain Senderens was barely twenty
when he came to Paris to learn his lessons
at the Tour d'Argent and at Lucas Carton.
He gained renown at l'Archestrate before taking over, in 1987,
the same Lucas Carton that had seen his debut.
His guiding words are rediscover, invent, create.

Before I go on to practical recipes, allow me to tell you why I love cooking, and why I am militant about a certain approach to gastronomy.

Rabelais, in *Manoir de Gaster* ("the worldly arts are our first master"), makes an analogy between food and birth. The lengthy gestation is both civilizing and liberating, leading us to discover our own means of measurement, which is our sense of taste. Tasting brings into play the soul, the heart, and the mind, action and thought. It asks that you examine the glass and the plate. In both the process of cooking and the making of wine, there is a passage from nature to culture. Tasting, as much as hearing or seeing, should be a technique akin to awakening; the lesson of gastronomy does not merely concern the primary pleasure that comes from appeasing a need. Science and feeling engender arrays of flavors as complex as arrangements of sounds, volumes, colors, or words. Gastronomy is different, but the emotion can be just as intense and transforming. It contains all the senses; it is a sum. Refinement in matters of the table and in conviviality can and should be learned, since as Brillat-Savarin said, "the knowledge of gastronomy is necessary to all men because it tends to augment the source of pleasure which awaits them," and "gastronomy is the rational knowledge of all that is connected to man insofar as it relates to eating."

Regarding aesthetics, cuisine that seeks harmony is not always tied to luxury (*luxus*: excess). There are those combinations, such as potatoes with herring (as long as you don't serve them with a hundred-dollar wine), which may be beneath notice (to some) but which can provide greater pleasure than a lobster that is no longer worth its price. Similarly, to honor your guests it is not indispensable that you serve a great wine if it is not appropriate to the dish. How many times have I seen, as I was about to taste a platter of seafood, with its underlying flavor of iodine, a Gewürztraminer, with its floral bouquet, served? Surely an example to avoid. All wines and foods when authentic and true, no matter where they come from, what they are, or how much they cost, merit our respect and our attention in matching them judiciously. It is from the harmonious blending of the moment, the dish, and the wine that genuine culinary emotion is born, due as much to the immediate pleasure as to the future joy of recollection.

Gastronomy is triply tied to the moment—its motto could be, with no irony intended, "here and now"—since it depends on:

—the evolution of society, with its taboos, the rejected and the accepted, through the interaction of religion, psychology, culture, nutrition, economy, geography, etc.;
—the seasons for their produce;
—the duration of the meal and the menu.

Unlike certain arts that please only one of the five senses, cuisine can delight each of them: vision through the ambience, the decor of the table, and the presentation of the dishes; smell through the scents and bouquets; taste through flavors and their harmonies; the sensation of touch in the mouth, through the texture of the food that gives it its consistency; and of hearing from the crunch of food.

From the concert of these components the immense pleasure of gastronomy is born, a unique and fleeting instant but a temporal pleasure indefinitely renewable. From the *nouvelle cuisine*—which died and was reborn as today's classic cuisine—new harmonies of flavor have issued to replace our cherished leg of lamb with flageolets or our squab with spring peas.

Let us leave room for Mr. Appetite—mentor to Gargantua—or to Panurge, who, according to learned etymology, signifies *le pain urge* (the bread beckons). *Bon appétit!*

PALATE
TEASERS

◆ ◆ ◆

There is nothing more dismissible
than those sinister little snacks
bought ready-made at the market.
Take the time to make your own.
Here is a list of ideas
that should inspire you with many others.

Remove the pits from green olives. Open a can of tuna in oil and drain it. Stir hard-cooked egg yolks into the tuna. Mash this with a fork; add a pinch of thyme and freshly ground pepper. Use it to stuff the olives. Use the same filling for cherry tomatoes, or spread it on marinated slices of small potatoes. Cook the potatoes in their jackets and then marinate them in a vinaigrette flavored with herbs.

You can also set marinated herring or chopped anchovies on these same potato slices.

Instead of the potatoes, use small canned artichoke bottoms, drained well and marinated in a vinaigrette. Cook some mussels and remove their shells. Boil the cooking liquid to reduce it to a few tablespoons, chill, stir in mayonnaise and chopped fresh herbs, then the mussels. Use the mixture to top the artichoke bottoms or scooped-out tomato halves.

Shell some hard-boiled quail eggs; cut off the top, remove the yolk, and cut off the bottom of each egg, making little cups that can stand upright on a plate. Fill them with a stuffing of your choice.

MINIATURE *CROQUE-MONSIEUR*

◆ ◆ ◆

Petits croque-monsieur

Serves 4

Butter

2 square slices of brioche-style bread, challah, or similarly enriched egg bread

1 slice of ham

2 tablespoons grated Gruyère cheese

Butter each slice of bread on one side. Place the ham on the buttered side of one slice, sprinkle with the Gruyère, and cover with the other slice, with the buttered side inside.

Cut off the outside crust of the sandwich. Heat up a sandwich maker or a *croque-monsieur* maker and place the sandwich inside. Cook about 3 minutes, until the bread is golden.

Alternatively, heat a small non-stick pan over moderately high heat. Cook the sandwich on one side until well toasted, turn over, and cook until the bread is golden and the cheese melted.

Cut the sandwich in 4. Serve hot, holding each piece together with a toothpick.

TARTLETS

◆ ◆ ◆

Petites tartelettes

12" tart pan

Serves 4 to 6

THE DOUGH

2 cups flour   About ⅓ cup ice water
Large pinch of salt
¾ cup butter, cut into small
    pieces

Sift together the flour and salt. Add the butter. Using your
hands or a pastry cutter, break up the butter in the flour until
the mixture is about as fine as rolled oats.

Add just enough ice water to moisten the flour. Toss to form
a rather dry dough. Do not overmix. Gather the dough together
and wrap in plastic film. Refrigerate at least 2 hours.

Preheat the oven to 400° F.

Roll out the dough to about ⅛ inch thick and with it line
a 12-inch tart pan; alternately, line an 11-inch-square pan with
the dough. Line the dough with aluminum foil and fill with
dried beans or pie weights. Bake for 10 minutes. Remove the
foil and weights and let cool.

Fill with one of the following mixtures.

When you have filled the tart, bake for 20 to 30 minutes,
until the filling is firm. Let cool to room temperature. To serve,
cut into wedges or squares.

QUICHE LORRAINE

◆ ◆ ◆

¼ pound sliced bacon
4 eggs
1½ cups *crème fraîche*
¼ pound Gruyère cheese,
    grated

Large pinch of nutmeg
Pepper and salt

Fry the bacon until it is cooked through but not crisp. Drain and chop coarsely. Stir together the eggs, *crème fraîche*, Gruyère, and bacon. Add the nutmeg and freshly ground pepper and salt. Be careful not to add too much salt on account of the bacon.

ONION TART

◆ ◆ ◆

2 tablespoons butter
5 medium-sized onions,
    sliced
4 eggs

1½ cups *crème fraîche*
Large pinch of nutmeg
Salt and pepper

Heat the butter in a large skillet over moderate heat. Add the onions and cook, stirring regularly, until they are soft and translucent and are just beginning to take on a golden hue, about 20 minutes.

Stir together the onions, eggs, *crème fraîche*, nutmeg, salt, and pepper.

SMOKED SALMON TART

♦ ♦ ♦

4 eggs

1½ cups *crème fraîche*

½ pound smoked salmon, diced

Ground cumin or juniper

Pepper and salt

Combine the eggs, *crème fraîche*, salmon, a large pinch of either the cumin or the juniper, the pepper, and just a little salt.

FRITTERS

♦ ♦ ♦

Beignets

1 ounce fresh yeast (or 1 tablespoon active dry yeast)

1 cup beer, at room temperature

Salt

1 cup flour

4 cups peanut oil

Shelled mussels, scallops, shrimp, crayfish, *escargots*

Prepare the batter ahead so that it has time to rise. Break up the yeast into a bowl, add the beer, and stir until combined. When the yeast is dissolved, add 2 pinches of salt and the flour and stir with a wooden spoon until smooth. Cover the bowl with a cloth and allow to rise 45 to 60 minutes.

Heat the oil to 370° F. in a deep fryer or a large heavy pan.

Utilizing one or more kinds of shellfish, pat the seafood dry, dip 2 pieces at a time in the batter, and then place them in the hot oil. You can fry about 8 fritters at a time. After about 3 minutes, they should be puffed and browned on one side. Carefully turn each fritter with a wooden spoon and continue cooking about 2 minutes longer. Remove the fritters with a slotted spoon and allow to drain on paper towels. Sprinkle lightly with salt.

Serve the hot fritters with mustard, ketchup, or mayonnaise enhanced with freshly chopped herbs, a little horseradish, or whatever one wishes.

For real gourmets, dry white wine (Jurançon, Vouvray, Sylvaner, Quincy, Chignin) is the best aperitif, along with Champagne, of course.

PRIMORDIAL SOUP

◆ ◆ ◆

While soup is a reflection of our land
and its bounty, it is also
one of the initial steps toward gastronomy.
It is when a boiled dish
takes the place of a roast
that a recipe is formulated
and transmitted.

◆◆

I n *The Origin of Table Manners*, Claude Lévi-Strauss established a parallel between boiling and civilization, seeing that boiled food is the result of a process twice mediated: once through the medium of water, in which you immerse the ingredients, and once again through the vessel, which contains both the solid and liquid ingredients. Inversely, the roast is subjected directly to the action of the fire. It thus remains in a "natural" state. It is also between roast and boiled that the recipe appears.

Originally, everything that was boiled was part of the woman's domain and was served in the restrained environment of the family or among friends. In contrast, the roast was made by men to celebrate a great feast or event, most notably to welcome a stranger. You can see where I'm headed: woman = culture; man = nature . . .

Claude Lévi-Strauss also believed that "one can boil meat that has previously been roasted, but cannot roast meat already boiled, since this would go against the current of history." According to this premise, the Romans and others would have been going against the current of history, since this latter practice was common through the Middle Ages.

Aristotle placed cooking by boiling before roasting because it seemed better suited to making a cooked dish out of raw meat. He wrote that "roast meat is more raw and drier than meat that is boiled." Already he perceived the opposition of the roasted and the boiled. Many Native American tribes associate the roast with living in the wild and the masculine, while the boiled is connected with village life and the feminine.

However, at the beginning of the nineteenth century, the gastronome Brillat-Savarin asserted that "boiled meat brings to mind flesh, its sauce less so . . ."

Little by little, the boiled dinner disappeared and our familiar soup, having become somewhat ordinary, was replaced by the *potage*, so much more feminine and sophisticated. Soon there followed a procession of *veloutés*, *bisques*, and *consommés*—refined dishes that are a far cry from the copious stews and abundant soups that came from the family pot.

Contrary to popular belief, boiling existed before the cooking vessel. Hollow trees or holes in rocks were once utilized as receptacles. The water was heated with the help of red-hot stones that were carried from the fire and immersed in the liquid, using a kind of giant wooden fork. Many signs of this have been found near ancient lakeside towns. In Austria there still exists a kind of tightly woven basket in which they cook in much the same way, without setting the container itself over the heat. It is surely from this practice that the cooking pot derives.

By boiling in water in a vessel, man brought food from the realm of nature to that of culture. Preparing food in this way leads to a genuine transformation of a raw ingredient, since boiling yields food that is usually very thoroughly cooked. From this instant, cooking came to indicate the cultural, intellectual, and technological level of a society.

THREE-BEAN SOUP

♦ ♦ ♦

*Soupe aux trois haricots
et au jarret fumé*

Serves 8 to 10

¾ cup dried black beans
¾ cup dried cannellini
¾ cup dried flageolet
2 smoked ham hocks (about
   1 pound in all)
2 large onions, chopped
5 garlic cloves, minced

1½ teaspoons dried thyme
1½ teaspoons ground cumin
Freshly ground black pepper
9 tablespoons *crème fraîche*
1 scallion, finely chopped
Salt

Rinse the beans under cold running water, then cover with
8 cups of water and let soak overnight.

Place the ham hocks in a large flameproof casserole with
3½ quarts of water. Bring to a brisk boil and cook for about
20 minutes.

Drain the beans and add to the casserole. Continue boiling
for an additional 15 minutes, stirring occasionally and skim-
ming off the foam that forms on the surface.

Add the onions, garlic, thyme, cumin, and pepper. Lower
the heat and cook for 1½ to 2 hours at a slow simmer, stirring
occasionally, until the beans are very tender.

In the meantime, stir together the *crème fraîche* and scallion
and set aside.

When the beans are cooked, remove the casserole from the
heat. Take out the ham hocks. When they are cool enough to
handle, separate the meat from the skin and bones. Cut the
meat in small pieces and add to the soup. Adjust the seasoning.

To serve, decorate the center of each bowl with a tablespoon
of the scallion cream.

Wines: A red Saint-Joseph-de-Bourgueil or a red Saint-Joseph

ROAST PUMPKIN

bake
2 hours

◆ ◆ ◆

Potiron rôti

Most pumpkins sold in the United States are rather bland and best suited for jack-o'-lanterns. Cooking pumpkins are much more flavorful if not as pretty. They tend to be squatter and paler in color, sometimes almost white.

Serves 4

4oz gruyere

1 cooking pumpkin (about 5 pounds)
½-pound loaf of French or Italian country-style bread
1 cup *crème fraîche*

¼ pound Gruyère cheese, grated
Salt and pepper
2 tablespoons melted butter

Rinse the outside of the pumpkin and wipe dry. Using a sharp knife, and cutting at a slight angle so that the tip of the knife is angled downward into the vegetable, cut off the top quarter of the pumpkin to form a lid. Using a large spoon, scrape out the seeds.

Cut the bread into thin slices and toast until golden brown. Set aside.

Preheat the oven to 425° F.

Line the pumpkin cavity with one layer of the bread, spread with 4 tablespoons of the *crème fraîche*, a quarter of the Gruyère, and a little salt and freshly ground pepper. Continue layering (4 layers in all), finishing with the Gruyère. Set the top back on the pumpkin.

Cut a piece of aluminum foil large enough to wrap the entire pumpkin. Brush the foil lightly with the butter. Wrap the pumpkin in the foil and place on a baking pan. Set in the oven and bake for about 2 hours. The pumpkin will be done when the outside skin has softened and a sharp knife can easily pierce through the skin to the interior flesh.

Remove from the oven, take off the foil, and place the pumpkin on a serving platter. Carefully remove the lid and, using a wooden spoon, stir the mixture inside, making sure to incorporate the pumpkin into the other ingredients. Taste for seasoning and add more salt and pepper if necessary. Serve very hot.

Wine: Gamay de Touraine

CHESTNUT SOUP WITH *CÈPES* AND APPLE

◆ ◆ ◆

*Soupe de châtaignes aux cèpes
et pommes fruits à la cannelle*

Serves 4 to 6

1½ pounds fresh chestnuts
1 ounce dried *cèpes* (*porcini*)
1 medium-sized leek
2 tablespoons vegetable oil
 or goose fat
2 garlic cloves, minced
1 onion, chopped

4–5 cups chicken broth
1 cup heavy cream
Salt and white pepper
½ large apple (Granny
 Smith or Northern Spy)
1 tablespoon butter
½ teaspoon cinnamon

Using a serrated knife, slit the skin of each chestnut. Bring about 6 cups water to a rapid boil and add the chestnuts. Boil for 10 minutes. Drain the chestnuts and, with the aid of a small paring knife, remove both the exterior shell and the interior skin. (The hotter the chestnuts are, the easier they are to peel.)

Cover the mushrooms with 1 cup cool water and let soak for ½ hour. Drain, reserving the liquid, and carefully rinse off any sand. Pass the soaking liquid through a coffee filter to remove any dirt.

Cut off the dark green part of the leek and discard. Clean the leek thoroughly and cut it into ½-inch dice.

Heat the oil in a large flameproof casserole over moderate heat. Add the leek, garlic, and onion. Sauté 4 to 5 minutes, until the onion is translucent. Add the chestnuts, mushrooms, mushroom soaking liquid, and 4 cups of the chicken broth. Bring to a boil, reduce the heat to a simmer, and cook about 30 minutes, until the chestnuts are very soft. Ladle the soup into a blender or food processor and puree until smooth. Stir in the cream and add salt and pepper to taste. Add more chicken broth if the soup seems too thick.

Peel and core the half apple and cut into ½-inch dice. Heat the butter in a small frying pan over moderately high heat until it begins to turn brown, add the apple, and sauté for 2 to 3 minutes, until the pieces just begin to soften. Sprinkle with the cinnamon.

To serve, reheat the soup over moderate heat. Ladle into individual bowls, decorating each with the sautéed apple.

ONION SOUP

◆ ◆ ◆

Soupe à l'oignon

Onion soup is said to instantly dissipate drunkenness. That is why the French call it drunkard's soup (*soupe d'ivrogne*). Soup destined for this mission should not contain any cheese.

Serves 4

2 tablespoons butter	3 ounces grated Gruyère or
3 large onions, finely sliced	Parmesan cheese
4 cups water or beef broth	(optional)
4 slices country-style bread	Salt

Heat the butter in a heavy flameproof casserole over moderate heat. Add the onions and cook, stirring regularly, until the onions are well browned (but not burned!). Add the water or broth, cover the casserole, and simmer for 30 minutes. Set each piece of bread in a soup bowl. Cover each slice with a quarter of the cheese (if desired) and pour the hot soup over both. Should you add cheese to the soup, be careful not to add too much salt.

VARIATION: Toast the bread (it can be lightly buttered or rubbed with garlic), cover with the cheese, and melt the cheese under a broiler. Set these pieces of bread on top of the soup. You can also add a little white wine or Port to the soup.

◆◆◆◆◆◆◆◆◆◆◆◆◆◆◆◆◆◆◆◆◆◆◆◆◆◆◆◆◆◆◆◆◆◆◆◆

YELLOW AND WHITE

◆ ◆ ◆

The egg is an amiable intermediary.
It can be prepared in innumerable ways.
Two hundred years ago there were
already some six hundred recipes!
Today a single book would not suffice
to draw up a complete inventory.

◆◆

From early on, eggs were indispensable to pastry making, but it took a while for them to be used on a daily basis in cooking. Though there are traces of recipes that predate Pericles, it is with the Roman Apicius that eggs become integral to the culinary art, most notably in binding sauces or with cheese. All the same, there is little evidence of eggs served as a main dish or even of a recipe in which they are the principal element. No doubt such recipes existed, but they were not sufficiently unusual to be written down.

At the beginning of the nineteenth century, eggs were preserved in bran as well as in oil. It was said that they would keep fresh—and could even be eaten soft-boiled—for more than six months!

In the *grande cuisine classique*, the egg owed much to the Church. Those of us who cherish good food should be grateful, since, for our benefit, the Church relaxed the Lenten laws by permitting eggs up until Good Friday. In fact, eggs were once indispensable for binding many sauces, in meatless ragouts, and most certainly as one of the critical elements of pastry making.

The Christian tradition, in associating the gift of eggs with the Easter holiday, did nothing more than graft its own symbols onto a tradition of ancient beliefs. Several centuries earlier, the Romans used to celebrate the festival of Ceres at about the same time of year. Offerings to the harvest goddess consisted essentially of eggs, symbols of fertility and renewal. During the same season, the Persians used to offer eggs as a propitiatory gift in order to attract the goodwill of others. In France, some wanted to establish this custom after the return of Louis VII from the Second Crusade in 1149. He received a huge number of gifts, and among them were so many eggs that he had them painted red and distributed among the people. This occurred at Easter and became a tradition that endured over three hundred years. Nevertheless, Louis XI, worried by such waste, forbade the consumption of eggs during Lent.

La Cuisine bourgeoise (1784) contains the best recipe for soft-boiled eggs: "When the water is ready, set them in it to boil for two minutes, remove them from the fire, cover for one minute to let them make their milk, and serve in a napkin."

Here, humorously summarized in 1925 by Georges Barbarin—founder of the *Revue des lettres* and curator of the Museum of Chinon—are all the ways of cooking an egg: "Two fried eggs: What a flat chest! Scrambled eggs: till death us do part. A soft-boiled egg: he has the right to his very own seat, like a person of note. I break open his skull while he is seated and adroitly operate on his eye for a cataract. Once the film is removed, the pupil appears. At times it is light yellow, at other times dark yellow. Being a cynic, I take it with a big pinch of salt. A hard-boiled egg: this cannonball may reek of sulfur. An omelette cast into the pan like a net: it catches in its golden mesh the flocking connoisseurs. Conjugation: you slobber, she slobbers, we slobber. A poached egg: though it be inoffensive, crouching on its plate, you will cruelly burst its belly. Its yellow blood flows, a brighter red, through its open wound, and you stem that flow with the weak pressure of a piece of bread. Beaten egg whites: snow and lilies, peak and flower, they are virginity itself. You could say a mouthful of cloud. It isn't possible, says the black hen, that this came out of my rear end."

OMELETTE DE LA MÈRE POULARD

◆ ◆ ◆

This is the famous recipe from Mont-Saint-Michel as revealed by Anne Grandclément in a lovely little book on the famous inn. Use 2 eggs per person. You will need a good wood fire. For each omelette, beat the eggs in a copper bowl set on a dishcloth that you have folded in quarters. Beat the eggs with a whisk, with a syncopated rhythm. It's said the tempo should be like a rumba. This should take 4 minutes. The mixture is ready when it has the consistency of crêpe batter. Heat 3 tablespoons butter in a long-handled omelette pan until the butter foams. Pour in the eggs and make the omelette.

Wine: A Montlouis demi-sec or a red Coteaux-d'Aix-en-Provence

EGGS COCOTTE

◆ ◆ ◆

Oeufs Cocotte

Serves 1

Butter   2 eggs
Salt and pepper   2 tablespoons heavy cream

    Butter a 3-inch ramekin and sprinkle the bottom with salt and pepper. Break the eggs into the dish.
    Preheat the oven to 375° F. Set the ramekin in a larger pan,

fill this pan with boiling water to halfway up the sides of the ramekin, and bake until the whites are firm but the yolks still runny (about 10 minutes). Heat the cream and pour over the eggs. You could also add chopped herbs, truffle juice, or truffle shavings.

Wine: A red Fiefs Vendéens such as Mareuil

A SHELL
DIVINE

◆ ◆ ◆

Did you know that
scallops are hermaphrodites?
The coral exhibits a gray part, which is the male organ,
and an orange part, more or less dark,
which is the female organ.
Should you eat the coral, or refrain?
The gourmets are divided.

Unlike most other mollusks, the scallop is a vagabond. It propels itself by expelling water, by rapidly opening and closing its top valve. Is this why, in France, it has been called *vanne* ("sluice gate or valve") or *pèlerine* ("pilgrim"), and, in the English-speaking nations, "scallop" or "pilgrim"? Scallops are, in fact, the symbol of the pilgrims on their way to Santiago (Saint James) de Compostela. (*The French term for scallops is co-quilles Saint-Jacques, literally Saint James shells.*)

The regulated scallop harvest takes place in France between mid-October and mid-May. When you buy scallops in the shell, pick ones that are heavy and tightly closed. At other times of the year, you can be assured that you are buying frozen scallops. The cultivation of scallops is still at an experimental stage and has yet to be perfected. These techniques have come to France from the United States, like the cultivation of clams.

RAW SCALLOPS

◆ ◆ ◆

Saint-Jacques crues

Due to its extreme simplicity, this recipe demands that you use not only the very freshest scallops but also an extra-virgin olive oil of the finest quality. The flavor of each raw ingredient must emerge.

Serves 4 as an appetizer

½ pound scallops	Freshly ground black pepper
4 tablespoons extra-virgin olive oil	Chopped fresh chives (optional)

Rinse the scallops in cold water and dry with paper towels. Chop them moderately fine.

Brush each of 4 chilled plates with a little of the olive oil. Set a mound of the scallops on each plate. Drizzle the remaining olive oil over the scallops and sprinkle with a little black pepper or, if you prefer, sprinkle lightly with chopped fresh chives. Serve with thin slices of white toast.

Wine: Saint-Péray

SCALLOPS IN *FILO*
WITH MUSHROOM CREAM SAUCE

◆ ◆ ◆

Saint-Jacques en phillo
à la crème de champignons

Serves 4

¼ pound shiitake
 mushrooms
¼ pound mushrooms or
 fresh *cèpes* (*see page 159*)
2 tablespoons butter
1½ cups heavy cream
1 teaspoon lemon juice

Salt and white pepper
16 medium-sized sea scallops
6–8 sheets *filo*
Melted butter
Julienned raw carrots
Chopped fresh chives

Clean the mushrooms by brushing off any dirt and cut into thin slices. Melt the butter in a large non-reactive skillet over moderate heat. Add the mushrooms and cook gently so that they do not brown. When the liquid the mushrooms have given off evaporates, add the cream, bring to a steady simmer, and reduce by half. Pour through a strainer, pressing down on the mixture to extract as much liquid as possible. Discard the mushrooms. Add the lemon juice and salt and pepper to taste.

Preheat the oven to 525° F.

Leave the scallops out for 10 minutes so that they come to room temperature. Drain them, pat dry with paper towels, and sprinkle lightly with salt and pepper. Cut the sheets of *filo* into 5-inch triangles. Place each scallop near the top of a triangle, pull the dough over to enclose the scallop, then pull the other 2 corners together and press to seal.

Brush the *filo*-wrapped scallops with a little melted butter and bake for 4 minutes.

To serve, spoon a quarter of the sauce onto each of 4 warm plates. Sprinkle with raw carrots cut into slivers (julienned) and with chopped fresh chives. Set the scallops in the center of each plate.

Wine: Meursault

SCALLOPS WITH VEGETABLES

◆ ◆ ◆

Saint-Jacques aux petits légumes

Serves 4

1 leek	¼ pound mushrooms
5 shallots	½ cucumber
1 medium-sized onion	2 teaspoons lemon juice
1 tablespoon butter	1 teaspoon chopped dill
⅓ cup white wine	*Beurre blanc (see Appendix)*
2 tablespoons Cognac	Salt and white pepper
20 large sea scallops	Chervil leaves
2 small carrots	

Slice the leek fine and clean it. Chop the shallots and onion. Heat the butter in a large non-reactive, flameproof casserole over moderate heat. Add the leek, shallots, and onion and sauté until the onion is softened. Add ⅓ cup water, the white wine, and the Cognac. Simmer 15 minutes, then strain. Discard the vegetables.

Cook the scallops in the wine mixture until they are opaque on the outside but still rare on the inside. Drain the scallops.

Cut the carrots and mushrooms separately into ¼-inch dice. Peel and seed the half cucumber and dice the same way. Cook the carrots in the wine mixture, then strain and reserve the carrots. Sauté the mushrooms with 2 tablespoons of the wine mixture and the lemon juice and set aside.

Heat the scallops, dill, mushrooms, carrots, and cucumber in about ⅓ cup of the cooking liquid. Remove from the heat and stir in ⅓ cup *beurre blanc*. Adjust the seasoning. Spoon into bowls, decorate with chervil leaves, and serve.

Wine: White Châteauneuf-du-Pape

SCALLOPS TARTARE

◆ ◆ ◆

Tartare de Saint-Jacques

Serves 4

2 egg yolks
1 tablespoon strong Dijon
   mustard
⅓ cup olive oil
⅔ cup peanut oil
16 large sea scallops, cut
   into ¼-inch dice
1 tablespoon chopped basil
2 tablespoons chopped dill
½ tablespoon chopped
   parsley
½ tablespoon chopped
   chervil
2 tablespoons chopped
   chives
3 medium-sized tomatoes,
   peeled, seeded, and diced
Juice of 1 lemon
Tabasco sauce

Make a mayonnaise. Stir together the egg yolks and mustard. Incorporate the oils very gradually, beating with a whisk the whole time.

Mix the mayonnaise with the scallops, herbs, and tomatoes, seasoning with the lemon juice and 6 dashes of Tabasco.

If you wish, you can make the tartare spicier by adding more Tabasco.

Wine: White Saint-Joseph

A BASS RONDO

◆ ◆ ◆

Whether called loup *in the Mediterranean area,
or* loubine *along the Atlantic shore of France,
the sea bass is an exquisite if fragile fish.
It should not be scaled,
especially when poached or grilled whole.
Here are two summer recipes
that reveal all its subtlety.*

◆◆◆◆◆◆◆◆◆◆◆◆◆◆◆◆◆◆◆◆◆◆◆◆◆◆◆◆◆◆◆◆◆◆◆◆

Under the monarchy, the right to sell fish had to be purchased from the king or from a previous owner of this privilege. The occupation could be practiced only by men, although there were a few narrow exceptions, including widows, oldest daughters, or wives who could temporarily take care of business while their husbands were away on a pilgrimage. Some attributed the fear of entrusting this role to women to their excessively colorful way of speaking. After all, in the eighteenth century, under the Regency, were they not called *poissardes* (a word meaning both "fishwife" and "vulgar, loudvoiced woman")? Nevertheless, they earned the rare privilege of being received by the king, as well as of being present when the queen was in labor. Fish, at the time, were considered the property of the king, and his cooks could choose the best specimens available at the markets without paying for them.

SEA BASS COOKED IN A SALT CRUST WITH SEAWEED

◆ ◆ ◆

Bar à la coque de sel
et d'algues marines

Unless you happen to live near an area of the country where fresh seaweed is harvested, you will have to buy dried seaweed and rehydrate it. Dried seaweed of numerous varieties (wakame and dulse are two examples) is available in most health food stores. You will need about ¼ pound for the recipe. Simply cover it with cold water and soak about 1 hour. Do not use nori, the toasted seaweed used for sushi.

Serves 4

4 small striped bass, each about 1 pound, or 2 weighing 2 pounds each	4 sprigs of thyme
Salt	4 sprigs of dill
4 sprigs of parsley	4½ pounds coarse salt
	1 pound seaweed

Preheat the oven to 500° F.

Lightly season the interior of each fish with the fine salt and insert the herbs. Line 2 roasting pans with a little less than half of the coarse salt. Sprinkle with enough water to moisten the salt. Arrange half the seaweed on top and then place the fish on the seaweed. Cover with the remaining seaweed and then the remaining salt. Moisten with a little more water and then press the fish package down with your hands.

Set in the preheated oven and bake for 12 to 15 minutes, depending on the size of the fish. Let it rest for 5 minutes after you take it out of the oven. Break the salt crust with a knife and remove the fish. Serve.

You may wish to serve the fish with Hollandaise Sauce.

HOLLANDAISE SAUCE

◆ ◆ ◆

Makes about 1½ cups

2 egg yolks
10 tablespoons softened
  butter
½ cup olive oil

Salt
Cayenne pepper to taste
Juice of ½ lemon

Combine the egg yolks with 3 tablespoons water in a metal bowl and beat over a very low flame or simmering water until the mixture is thick and foamy. Over the very low heat, add the butter, tablespoon by tablespoon, making sure it is fully incorporated between each addition. Beat in the olive oil a little at a time. Season with salt, the Cayenne, and the lemon juice.

Wine: White Châteauneuf-du-Pape

GRILLED SEA BASS

WITH FENNEL

◆ ◆ ◆

Bar grillé au fenouil

To make the sauce, you will need to use an electric juicer. Alternately, your neighborhood health food store may be willing to make fennel juice for you.

Serves 4

5 coriander seeds	1 small onion
5 white peppercorns	1½ tablespoons butter
2 bay leaves	1 red bell pepper
¼ teaspoon coarse salt	1 green bell pepper
2 large sprigs of thyme	2 cups *crème fraîche*
2 garlic cloves	¾ pound mushrooms
6 plum tomatoes	Juice of 1 lemon
Olive oil	1 star anise
3 fennel bulbs	1½ pounds sea bass fillet
Salt and pepper	¼ cup peanut oil

Preheat the oven to 225° F.

Crush the coriander and reserve separately. Crush the peppercorns, bay leaves, coarse salt, thyme, and garlic and combine. Core the tomatoes, cut in half lengthwise, and remove the seeds. Arrange the tomato halves on a baking sheet, rub the insides with the spice-garlic mixture, and brush lightly with olive oil. Bake in the preheated oven for 3 hours.

Wash 2 of the fennel bulbs and cut off and reserve their stalks. Plunge the 2 bulbs into boiling water, return the water to a boil, remove the fennel, and drain. Place the bulbs in a small casserole that just holds them, cover with olive oil (you will need 2 to 3 cups), season with salt and pepper, and bake, covered, for 3 hours at 225° F.

Chop the onion and sauté in a little butter. Cut the 2 peppers into small dice and add to the onions. Add 1¼ cups of the *crème fraîche*, bring to a boil, and cook for about 10 minutes, until thickened.

Wash, drain, and dice the mushrooms. Sauté over high heat with a little butter until all the water has evaporated. Add the remaining ¾ cup *crème fraîche* and the coriander. Season with salt and pepper and continue cooking for 10 minutes.

Chop the remaining fennel bulb and fennel stalks and combine with the lemon juice and star anise. Using an electric vegetable juicer, extract the juice from this mixture. Pour ⅓ cup into a small saucepan over low heat.

Cut the bass fillet into 4 pieces and brush lightly with olive oil. Grill or broil for about 6 minutes.

In a blender, combine the warm fennel juice with ¼ cup olive oil and the peanut oil. Add salt and pepper to taste.

To serve, set a piece of bass in the center of each plate. Place 3 tomato halves around the fish, spoon the pepper mixture on top. Between the tomato halves place pieces of the braised fennel and top them with the mushrooms. On each plate, spoon the fennel sauce around the fish.

Wine: White Châteauneuf-du-Pape

A DEVILISH
DELIGHT

◆ ◆ ◆

The lotte has a flaccid body devoid of scales,
and an enormous jaw
that has led the French to dub it
diable de mer, or "devil of the sea."
In France it is sold as lotte,
in America as monkfish.
It is delectable.

◆◆◆◆◆◆◆◆◆◆◆◆◆◆◆◆◆◆◆◆◆◆◆◆◆◆◆◆◆◆◆◆◆◆◆◆◆◆◆

The fish that we encounter in French fish markets under the name *lotte* or *queue de lotte* (*lotte* tail) is identical to the fish called *baudroie*. It is so ugly, its appearance so unappealing with its flaccid, scaleless body and its enormous head and jaw, that it has been called *crapaud* ("toad") or *diable de mer* ("devil of the sea"). This is why the fish in its entirety is unknown to the consumer, who always encounters it on the fish counter already skinned and with its head removed.

"Notwithstanding its failings according to the canons of elementary aesthetics," as F. Amunatequin remarked (*La Cuisine du terroir* by R. Courtine), monkfish is lean, boneless, delicate, yet firm and of high quality. It is cooked somewhat like meat. Furthermore, the fish, which yields so little waste, is easy to work with.

The word *baudroie* is associated with the South of France and makes the fish seem more elegant. *Bourride à la sétoise* (unlike other recipes of this kind) contains no other fish but monkfish. (It is always called *baudroie*, never *lotte*, in Sète, the birthplace of the folk singer Georges Brassens, as well as the town where a tired gatekeeper once trained his dog to conduct tourists to the tomb of the poet Paul Valéry.)

And while the early-twentieth-century writer Charles Maurras preferred *bouillabaisse*, the late-nineteenth-century novelist Alphonse Daudet did not disdain the "creamy milk" that is *bourride*.

BOURRIDE

◆ ◆ ◆

Use at least three types of white-fleshed fish on the bone in any proportion for this recipe. Among the possibilities are striped bass, mullet, whiting, monkfish, and ocean perch.

Serves 4

1 leek	Salt and pepper
1 onion	4½ pounds white-fleshed
1 fennel bulb	fish
1 carrot	3 garlic cloves
2 sprigs of thyme	5 egg yolks
2 bay leaves	2 cups olive oil
Rind of 1 orange	Lemon juice (optional)
2 cups dry white wine	

Slice and clean the leek. Slice the onion, fennel, and carrot. Combine these vegetables with 4 cups water, the thyme, bay leaves, orange rind, and wine in a large non-reactive, flameproof casserole. Season with salt and pepper. Bring to a boil and simmer 15 minutes. Cut the fish into large pieces, add to the pot, cover, bring to a boil, and simmer for about 10 minutes, until the fish is barely cooked through. Remove the fish pieces and strain the broth.

Make an *aïoli*. In a mortar or food processor, crush the garlic and add 2 of the egg yolks. Season with salt. Little by little, drop by drop, incorporate the olive oil. Add a little lemon juice if you wish. Set aside a third and put the rest in a large flameproof casserole. Stir in the remaining egg yolks. Place the casserole over low heat and slowly stir in the fish broth. Make sure the broth is well incorporated. Do not allow it to boil. Serve with large croutons made from coarse white peasant bread.

Serve the fish as a second course with the remaining *aïoli*.

Wine: Cassis or a Provençal rosé

BOURRIDE À LA SÉTOISE

◆ ◆ ◆

Serves 4

2 carrots	¾ cup olive oil
2 leeks	2½ pounds monkfish
3 celery stalks	Salt and pepper
1 large beet leaf (or Swiss chard)	1 egg yolk
	1 garlic clove, crushed
2 tomatoes, seeded and peeled	Lemon juice

Chop fine the carrots, leeks, celery, beet leaf, and tomatoes. Heat about 2 tablespoons of the olive oil in a large flameproof casserole over moderately low heat. Add the chopped vegetables and sauté for 10 minutes.

Cut the monkfish into pieces, set on top of the vegetables, cover the casserole tightly, and cook over low heat for about 20 minutes. Season with salt and pepper.

Make a mayonnaise by combining the egg yolk and crushed garlic and slowly incorporating about ⅔ cup of the olive oil. Season with salt, pepper, and lemon juice

To serve, set the monkfish on a warm deep platter. Cover with the vegetable sauce. Serve the mayonnaise on the side.

Wine: Coteaux-du-Languedoc

MONKFISH À LA PALAVASIENNE

◆ ◆ ◆

Gigot de mer à la palavasienne

Serves 4

3 tablespoons olive oil
3 medium-sized onions
½ pound eggplant
½ pound zucchini
½ pound tomatoes, peeled
Salt and pepper
Bouquet garni (2 sprigs of
   thyme, 2 sprigs of parsley,
   2 bay leaves, tied
   together)

3 large garlic cloves
2 pounds monkfish, in one
   piece
½ teaspoon powdered thyme
¼ teaspoon powdered
   rosemary
¾ cup white wine

To make the *ratatouille*, heat 1½ tablespoons of the olive oil in a flameproof casserole over moderate heat. Slice 2 of the onions and add. Slice the eggplant and zucchini and add. Cook until the vegetables begin to brown, about 10 minutes. Add the tomatoes, salt, pepper, and *bouquet garni*. Cook, covered, for 20 minutes over moderate heat.

Cut 2 of the garlic cloves into 10 slivers each. Using a small sharp knife, make slits in the monkfish and insert a sliver of garlic in each, making sure none of the garlic sticks out. Do this all over the fish at evenly spaced intervals.

Chop the remaining garlic and slice the remaining onion. Heat the remaining olive oil in a large flameproof casserole over moderately high heat. Add the monkfish and brown lightly on all sides. Take out the fish and add the chopped garlic and onion, the thyme, rosemary, and wine to the same casserole. Replace the fish, cover, and cook over moderately low heat for about 45 minutes.

To serve, spoon the *ratatouille* onto a warm platter. Set the monkfish on top. Boil the cooking juices to reduce by half. Strain and pour over the fish.

Wine: White Châteauneuf-du-Pape

MONKFISH WITH SAFFRON

◆ ◆ ◆

Lotte au safran

Serves 4

1 pound leeks	1 tablespoon olive oil
Aïoli (2 garlic cloves, 1 egg yolk, 1 cup olive oil)	1 cup fish broth
1½ pounds monkfish fillet	¼ teaspoon saffron threads
Salt and pepper	1 teaspoon chopped fresh chives

Slice and wash the leeks. Bring 4 cups water to a boil; add a little salt and the leeks. Cook the leeks for 20 minutes. Drain and cool under cold running water.

Make the *aïoli* as in the recipe for *Bourride* (page 50).

Cut the monkfish into ¾-inch slices. Season with salt and pepper. Heat the olive oil in a large skillet, add the fish, and cook until the fish is lightly browned and cooked through.

Combine the fish broth and saffron in a saucepan. Boil until reduced by half. Remove from the heat and whisk in the *aïoli*.

Arrange the leeks in a dome shape on a platter, set the fish on top, and pour the sauce around the center. Decorate with the chives.

Wine: Condrieu or Tokay or Pinot Gris d'Alsace

MONKFISH WITH

LEMON GRASS

◆ ◆ ◆

Lotte à la citronnelle

The recipe calls for lemon grass, which is available in Asian markets, especially those catering to a Thai, Vietnamese, or Filipino clientele. Quatre-épices is a common French spice mixture, which you can make by combining 1 part cinnamon, 1 part allspice, 1 part cloves, and 1 part nutmeg.

Serves 4

¼ pound black Chinese
    mushrooms
½ pound carrots
1 pound snow peas
2 stalks of lemon grass
1½ pounds monkfish fillet
Salt and pepper

⅓ cup soy sauce
¾ cup dry sherry
¾ cup hard cider
¼ teaspoon *quatre-épices*
1 teaspoon chopped fresh
    ginger
⅓ pound bean sprouts

Soak the mushrooms in warm water for 1 hour, drain well, remove and discard the stems, then slice fine. Slice the carrots and string the snow pea pods. Chop the lemon grass very fine.

Bring a large pot of salted water to a boil and separately cook the carrots and snow peas until barely done. Drain and cool.

Cut the monkfish into thin slices. Steam for 3 to 4 minutes. Season with salt and pepper.

Combine the soy sauce, sherry, cider, *quatre-épices*, lemon grass, and ginger. Set half aside. Heat the remainder over low heat. Add the carrots, snow peas, mushrooms, and finally the bean sprouts and cook until heated through. Heat the remainder of the sauce.

Arrange the vegetables on a platter, set the monkfish on top, and spoon the reserved sauce over the fish.

Wine: White Hermitage

PRESERVING
SALMON

◆ ◆ ◆

*Salmon were once abundant in French rivers,
and some servants' contracts used to stipulate
that they would not have to
eat salmon more than twice a week.
Times have changed.
Salmon has come up in the world.*

Salmon is a migrating fish that alternates parts of its life cycle between fresh water (during reproduction, laying of eggs, and the early stages of growth) and salt water (during the later stages of growth and as an adult).

Pollution and the poor upkeep of our streams and dams that prevent the salmon (even when helped out by "ladders") from returning to their spawning grounds have reduced the catch considerably in France, to the profit of foreign salmon (from Scotland, Denmark, Norway, and so on), as well as of salmon farming.

Its fine and unctuous flesh makes it an exceptional choice for connoisseurs. Be aware, nonetheless, that although all salmon belong to one family, the Salmonidae, they are divided between two genera. *Salmo salar*, the Atlantic salmon, is the best. Avoid the second-rate *Oncorhynchus*, the Pacific salmon, which, in France, you commonly find in the form of commercial smoked salmon (often much redder and often falsely labeled "king") or in cans.

Smoked salmon is a refined dish which, more and more, is occupying a position of honor on every table.

Very early, man sought to ensure that his foods would be well preserved. He understood, without knowing why at the time, that one of the means (and secrets) consisted of isolating food from air, light, and humidity by covering it with clay, honey, vinegar, or fat; or else he chose a system that modified an aspect of the taste through ashes, salting, smoking, or drying. Historically, the Sumerians were the first to utilize all these procedures.

Traditionally, smoked salmon is always served as is, with rye bread or blinis and lemon. Above all, don't forget a little freshly ground pepper.

BAKED POTATO
WITH SMOKED SALMON

◆ ◆ ◆

Pomme de terre à notre façon

Serves 1

1 large baking potato	⅓ cup butter
¾ cup dry white wine	3 tablespoons heavy cream
2 shallots, chopped	1 thick slice of smoked
2 tablespoons plus	salmon
1 teaspoon white wine	1 sprig of dill, chopped
vinegar	2 eggs

Wrap the potato in foil and bake in a 325° F. oven for about 45 minutes, or until a sharp knife penetrates it easily.

Combine the white wine, shallots, and 2 tablespoons vinegar in a small non-reactive saucepan and boil until the liquid has reduced to about 2 tablespoons. Over very low heat, whisk in the butter, a small piece at a time. Continue to stir until all of the butter has liquefied. Stir in the heavy cream. Remove from the heat. Dice the salmon and add to the sauce along with the dill.

Bring about 3 cups water to a bare simmer; add 1 teaspoon vinegar. Slip the eggs into the simmering water and poach until the whites are set and the yolks are still liquid. Remove with a slotted spoon.

Slit the potato and open it up to form a cavity. Set the potato on a plate, slip the eggs into the cavity, and cover with the salmon sauce.

Wine: A dry Jurançon

WARM SMOKED SALMON

WITH CAVIAR

◆ ◆ ◆

Saumon fumé chaud au caviar

You can substitute clam juice for the fish broth in the recipe.

Serves 1

1 small strip lime zest	1 teaspoon chopped celery
2 thin slices ginger root, peeled	2 thick slices of smoked salmon (about 2 ounces each)
1 shallot, chopped	
⅓ cup Champagne	½ teaspoon chopped dill
⅓ cup fish broth	½ teaspoon osetra sturgeon caviar
⅓ cup heavy cream	
5 tablespoons butter	12 grains salmon caviar
8 thin slices of cucumber	

Slice the lime zest and ginger into very thin slivers. Plunge into boiling water for 30 seconds, drain, and cool under cold running water.

Preheat the oven to 300° F.

Combine the shallot and Champagne in a small non-reactive saucepan, and boil until virtually no liquid remains. Add the fish broth and repeat the procedure. Add the cream and boil to reduce by half. Set over very low heat. Whisk in the butter, a small piece at a time. Continue to stir until all of the butter has liquefied. Strain through a fine sieve.

Toss the lime zest, ginger, cucumber, and celery and arrange in a small pile in the center of a plate.

Brush the smoked salmon very lightly with melted butter and set in the preheated oven for about 3 minutes so that it is just barely warmed through. Arrange it on the vegetables. Stir the dill and the two caviars into the sauce and spoon the sauce around the fish.

Wine: White Reuilly from the Loire

GRILLED SMOKED SALMON

WITH HORSERADISH AND CELERIAC

◆ ◆ ◆

Saumon fumé grillé au raifort et au céleri

Serves 4

1 pound celery root (celeriac), with stalks and leaves	1 teaspoon chopped dill
	2 cups heavy cream
	Peanut oil
2 cups milk	1¼ pounds smoked salmon, in one piece
1 teaspoon plus 1 tablespoon Dijon mustard	
1 teaspoon plus 2 tablespoons grated horseradish	1 large head of *frisée* or curly endive
Salt and white pepper	3 tablespoons vinaigrette (*see Appendix*)

Peel the celery root, cut into coarse dice, set in a small saucepan, add the milk, cover, bring to a boil, and simmer until very tender. Drain. Puree in a food processor or pass through a coarse sieve. Stir in 1 teaspoon of the mustard and 1 teaspoon of the horseradish and add salt and white pepper to taste. Keep warm. Just before serving, stir in the dill.

Pour the cream into a wide non-reactive saucepan and boil to reduce by half. While it is still boiling, stir in the remaining mustard and horseradish. Strain.

Remove the celery leaves from the stalk. Fill a heavy-bottomed saucepan to the depth of 1 inch with the oil. Set over moderately high heat. The fat should be so hot that the celery leaves immediately sizzle when you add them. Fry the celery leaves in batches until crisp. Drain well on paper towels.

Cut the salmon into 5 quarter-pound pieces. Reserve 4 and slice the fifth in thin strips. Toss the lettuce with the vinaigrette and the salmon strips.

Broil or grill the 4 salmon pieces briefly, just so that they are warmed through.

Arrange the salmon on 4 plates with the celery puree, the fried celery leaves, and the salad. Serve the sauce on the side.

Wine: Tokay d'Alsace

LONG LIVE
COD!

◆ ◆ ◆

You think cod banal?
You are misinformed.
Not only is it delicious, economical, dietetic,
and easy to cook but it can reveal
gastronomic surprises
that will make you forget
those slabs of frozen codfish.

◆◆◆

This large fish, which can measure up to 5 feet in length, is usually sold in thick slices or steaks. When it is salted, it is known as salt cod (*morue*, in French) and featured in innumerable recipes the world over.

Cod thrives in cold water (from 32° F. to 50° F.) and thus it is best caught in the waters off northern France, that is, north of Bordeaux. To the south, it is replaced by a smaller variety called *moruette*, or *doguette* in the Basque country. The flesh of codfish is marvelous toward the head; don't forget to ask for it at your fishmonger's. White, delicate, lightly resilient, it will not tolerate long cooking. If you cook it carefully, cod will flake and give off milky cooking juices. It is suitable for just about every method of preparation with the exception of grilling and is available year round. Moreover, it is a lean fish (68 calories per each 3½-ounce serving) and thus recommended for those on a diet.

Jean-Paul Aron, discussing the evolution of tastes in *Le Mangeur du XIXe siècle* (*Eating in the Nineteenth Century*), writes that at that period, mullet was considered the fish of choice, whereas today it is neglected. Personally, I have long considered cod superior to bass. This is in part because of the latter's lack of texture but, above all, the quality-price ratio, which weighs in on the side of cod. Alas, this is too clearly represented by the breaded fish cakes found in the supermarket freezer.

Here is a recipe that I have featured on my menu.

COD COOKED ON ITS SKIN

WITH HERB-SMOTHERED POTATOES

◆ ◆ ◆

Cabillaud cuit sur la peau aux pommes de terre émiettées à la fondue d'herbes

Serves 4

1 small beet, cooked (*see page 186*)
2 lemons
2 bunches of chives
1 small bunch of parsley
15 basil leaves
1 thin slice salt pork (about 2 ounces)
1 teaspoon mustard
12 tablespoons butter, softened
Salt and white pepper
¾ pound small red potatoes
4 pieces cod fillet, with skin, each about ½ pound
1½ tablespoons olive oil

Cut the beet into thin julienne strips. Using a vegetable peeler, peel the yellow zest from the 2 lemons. Slice the zest as thin as possible. Plunge it into boiling water for 30 seconds, then drain and cool under cold running water.

Chop all the herbs fine, and set aside about 1 teaspoon of the chives. Chop the salt pork fine. Stir the herbs, salt pork, and mustard into the butter, then press this herb butter through a sieve 3 times. Season with salt and pepper.

Preheat the oven to 375° F.

Boil the potatoes in their jackets in lightly salted water until tender. Drain, peel, and mash coarsely with a fork.

Sprinkle the cod lightly with salt and pepper. Heat the olive oil in a large heavy skillet with an ovenproof handle over moderately high heat. Add the cod fillets, skin side down, and cook 2 minutes. Place the pan in the oven and continue to cook an additional 2 minutes. The skin should be very crisp. Remove from the oven and let sit in the pan.

Mix the beet, lemon zest, and reserved chives. Set a piece of the cod, skin side up, in the center of each plate. Place the potatoes beside the cod and top the potatoes with a dollop of the herb butter. Arrange the beet mixture on either side of the cod and potatoes.

POACHED COD WITH A CREAMY SAUCE OF MUSTARD, LEEKS, LEMON ZEST, AND FRESH CORIANDER

◆ ◆ ◆

Cabillaud poché avec crème de moutarde, poireaux, zeste de citron, et coriandre fraîche

Serves 4

2 cups milk
Salt
4 codfish steaks, each about
  ½ pound
5 leeks
3 tablespoons butter
Freshly ground white pepper

1 lemon
½ cup heavy cream
1–2 tablespoons Dijon
  mustard
½ cup loosely packed
  coriander leaves

Combine the 2 cups milk with 2 cups water in a non-reactive pan large enough to hold the 4 cod steaks side by side. Season with salt. Bring to a boil, add the cod, return to a boil, then turn off the heat. Let the fish rest in the poaching liquid for 3 minutes, until just cooked through.

In the meantime, slice the white parts of the leeks and wash thoroughly. Heat 1 tablespoon of the butter in a skillet over moderately low heat. Add the leeks, season with salt and pepper, and cook for about 10 minutes. Using a vegetable peeler, peel the yellow zest from the lemons. Slice the zest as thin as possible. Plunge it into boiling water for 30 seconds, then drain and cool under cold running water. Add the cream to the leeks, bring to a boil, and cook until it is reduced by half. Stir in mustard according to taste, remove the pan from the heat, and then incorporate the remaining butter. Add the lemon zest. Adjust the seasoning.

Remove the cod from the poaching liquid, remove the skin and bones, and set 2 fillets on each plate. Stir the coriander leaves into the sauce and spoon the sauce over the fish.

COD WITH EGGPLANT ''CAVIAR''

◆ ◆ ◆

Cabillaud au caviar d'aubergine

Serves 4

1 teaspoon wine vinegar
1 teaspoon sherry vinegar
3 tablespoons peanut oil
¼ teaspoon caraway seed
Salt and pepper
4 medium eggplants, about
   3 pounds in all
¾ cup olive oil
1 large red bell pepper
1 small green bell pepper
8 medium-sized mushrooms
1 medium-sized tomato (or
   ½ cup drained canned
   tomato)

2 shallots
1 large garlic clove
2 anchovy fillets
2 pounds cod, in one piece
1 fresh bay leaf
4 sprigs of fresh thyme
4 teaspoons chopped mixed
   herbs (chervil, parsley,
   chives)

Stir together the 2 vinegars and peanut oil with the caraway seed. Season with salt and pepper.

Preheat the oven to 400° F.

Place the whole eggplants in a roasting pan, rub with 4 tablespoons of the olive oil, and roast in the preheated oven for about 1 hour 15 minutes. Let cool and peel. Squeeze as much water out of the pulp as possible and chop. Remove the seeds and stems from the peppers and cut into ¾-inch dice. Cut the mushrooms in quarters. Peel the tomato, squeeze out the seeds, and dice. Chop the shallots, garlic clove, and anchovy fillets. Put the peppers, mushrooms, tomato, shallots, garlic and anchovy in a large shallow pan with 4 tablespoons of the olive oil. Cook over moderate heat for about 15 minutes, stirring occasionally. Add the eggplant and mix. Season with salt and pepper to taste.

Preheat the oven to 450° F.

Place the bay leaf and thyme in the cavity of the cod, set in a roasting pan, and rub with the remaining olive oil. Roast for about 15 minutes, turn, and continue cooking for an additional 15 minutes, or until cooked through. Remove the skin and bones from the cod. Reheat the eggplant "caviar" and add the chopped herbs. To serve, place the codfish on top of the caviar. If necessary, reheat briefly in the oven. Finally spoon the caraway vinaigrette over the fish.

ROASTING:
THE ART AND
THE CRAFT

◆ ◆ ◆

"You may be born a cook,
but you must learn to roast," asserted Brillat-Savarin.
It was his way of emphasizing that roasting
demands knowledge and careful attention.
From the cooking to the carving—
by way of the gravy—here is my advice.

◆◆

To roast meat or poultry is to expose it to very high heat (475° F. to 500° F.) so that it will brown and the juices in the interior will be conserved. The piece of meat should be salted and lightly oiled (about 1 tablespoon per pound, using 2 parts oil to 1 part butter). Place it in a pan, but never directly, so that it doesn't cook in its grease. Set it on coarsely chopped bones, onions and carrots, or, better yet, on a roasting rack.

Once the meat has begun to brown, baste it with the fat that has gathered in the pan and sprinkle lightly with pepper. Reduce the temperature—this will depend on the cooking time: generally to about 375° F. Do not hesitate to baste the roast every 10 minutes and to season it.

The initial shock during browning draws the blood toward the interior of the roast and makes it contract. If you carve the meat immediately afterward, the outside will be well cooked but gray and the inside will be very rare. Above all, the meat will be stiff. You therefore need to let it rest in a warm place covered with aluminum foil or with a bowl. In this way, through capillary action, the blood will return toward the exterior, loosening the vessels and tenderizing the roast. You will then obtain an attractive uniform color: a tender red for beef and pink for lamb. In general, for large roasts, you need to allow about one half the cooking time for "resting"; for small roasts, about 5 to 10 minutes.

Avoid piercing the roast during cooking, since the blood and juices will be drawn out. Some particularly fragile or dry meats—veal or game—need to be wrapped in a thin layer of pork fat. This is called barding. The fat is removed a short time before the end of cooking to allow the roast to brown.

The success of a roast, once it is perfectly cooked, depends on the gravy. It should be neither too thin nor too thick, with just enough beads of fat to bring a smile of pleasure. In this field, the feminine touch is often superior to the male.

If the cooking was conducted with prudence, the pan will not be burned. For this reason, you should pick the right-sized pan for the roast: it should just be able to contain it. Halfway through cooking, add several garlic cloves and an unpeeled shallot or a quarter of an onion.

When the meat is cooked and resting in a warm place, let the pan juices that are suspended in the fat settle for about 5 minutes. Save no more than a quarter of the fat. Put the pan on the stove and add ½ cup water. Scrape the bottom while stirring with a metal spatula. Reduce the liquid by half, crush the garlic and shallot, and then strain this gravy into a sauce-boat. Before serving, place the roast in the oven for a few minutes and then carve. Don't forget to season each slice with salt and freshly ground pepper, since the exterior seasoning never penetrates completely.

Make sure you also heat the plates so that everything remains warm.

Which brings to mind the question: why do we heat our food and then why do we eat it hot? Desmond Morris informs us, at the end of *The Naked Ape*, that it is to simulate "the temperature of the prey." This brings us back not simply to our carnivorous state but, rather, to a more ancient past when we were hunters.

As a guide, here are some approximate cooking times. They necessarily depend on your oven and the thickness of the roast.

Beef rib roast: 15 minutes per pound
Leg of lamb: 15 minutes per pound
Veal: 22 minutes per pound
Duck: 5 minutes per pound
Squab: 10 to 12 minutes for a 1-pound bird
Chicken: 20 minutes per pound

Here is an idea for a side dish for your roast.

POTATO *GALETTE*

◆ ◆ ◆

Galette de pommes de terre

Serves 6 to 8

6 Idaho potatoes
5 egg yolks
Salt to taste

10 tablespoons butter,
softened

Bake the potatoes in a 325° F. oven for about 45 minutes, or until soft. Scoop out the pulp and measure 2½ cups. Stir in 4 egg yolks, one by one. Add salt to taste. Incorporate the butter. When the mixture is homogenous, form it into a ball and flatten it with the palm of your hand. Re-form the ball, flatten it again, then repeat this operation twice more.

Preheat the oven to 425° F.

Lightly butter a baking sheet. Set the potato mixture on the sheet and flatten to a thickness of about 1½ inches. Score the top with the tip of a knife, brush with the remaining egg yolk, and set in the oven until the *galette* is golden, about 20 minutes.

CHARTING
TENDERNESS

◆ ◆ ◆

Learn to talk to your butcher knowledgeably.
Discuss with him the flavor
of sirloin versus round.
Get to know the quality and the use of each cut and
the differences between cuts.
The following is a short guide to using beef.

Cattle have been domesticated for over forty centuries and beef cattle have become the butcher's animal *par excellence*. It seems that the ancestor of the butcher (*boucher* in French) was the Roman *buccarius*, who specialized in cutting up beef.

Beef provides a widely varied inventory of cuts for all tastes, pocketbooks, and cooking methods (and also for serving raw): rare steaks seared in a matter of minutes or long-simmered braises, to say nothing of the unequaled *boeuf gros sel* (boiled beef served with vegetables and coarse salt).

Beef butchering follows certain precise rules, but even without being a professional, it isn't too difficult to make sense of the jargon that assigns a name to each cut—that is, as long as you know what you want. Try to lose the habit of simply asking for a "really tender steak" or a "really juicy roast." Learn to recognize each cut, its characteristics, and its flavor.

Do not confuse quality with category. The category is determined by a cut's culinary destination: the first category for grilling or roasting, the second for braising, and the third for boiling.

THE INVENTORY OF BEEF*

Let's begin our inventory with the slice of meat intended for grilling or pan frying that we call a steak. The cuts among which you will choose belong to the first category, that is, meat meant to be cooked quickly. These are always the most sought after and expensive. The *filet* (tenderloin), which is cut into tournedos or the thicker Chateaubriands, is very tender and there is virtually no waste, much like the *romsteck* (rump steak or sirloin), which is very flavorful. The *faux-filet* (loin or New York strip steak) is also tender, but there is more waste. The same is true of the *entrecôte* (club steak), which is particularly tasty grilled or pan-fried. Choose one that is nice and thick, well marbled, and a little fatty on the outside.

Other cuts of the same type will satisfy the red meat devotee: *gîte à la noix* (eye of round), *tranche grasse* (bottom round) and *aiguillette* (top round). *Bavette d'aloyau* (flank steak), *hampe* (skirt steak), and *onglet* ("London broil") offer meat that is juicy if a little tougher than the cuts we have been discussing. However, they are very flavorful, especially if you serve them with a condiment such as shallots. Special mention should be made of the *araignée* (a piece taken from the round); this somewhat fatty cut, very tender and of irregular form, should be very carefully cleaned. It is very juicy when grilled and a delicious stand-in for steak.

All the meats intended for broiling or pan frying must be cooked quickly: from 4 to 8 minutes, depending on whether you want your meat very rare, medium rare, or well done.

---

* The French butcher meat very differently from Americans. The American equivalents (in parentheses) are only approximations and cannot always be substituted for the French cuts.

MOVING ON TO THE ROAST

You will find the same variety of cuts as for steaks. Choose among the *filet, faux-filet, romsteck, l'entrecôte, tranche grasse,* and *aiguillette* and don't forget the flavorful *côte de boeuf* (standing rib roast). You should discover the *tende-de-tranche* (eye of round), which is known as the "butcher's choice" and is reserved for real connoisseurs. Depending on its form, which can be elongated or compact, it is given imaginative names in French such as *limande* (lemon sole) or *merlan* (whiting), *boule-de-tende* (tender ball, or pear), and *rond-de-tende* (tender round, or large pear). The *araignée* can also be roasted. For all these meats, count on about 15 minutes' cooking time per pound.

Let's leave the first category now to discuss the second and the third categories: meat that will clearly require lengthier cooking. These cuts are braised or stewed, which is to say that they are first quickly seared and then simmered with wine or other liquid, such as water. For cooking a *daube, boeuf à la mode,* or *boeuf bourguignon* you can choose among six cuts. The *macreuse* (chuck) is tender enough, as is the *griffe* (from the chuck), noted for its flavor. *Gîte de jumeau* (chuck from the neck portion) is somewhat gelatinous and will thus make a rich broth. The same is true for *dessus de côtes* (boned short ribs), which have the advantage that there is little waste. *Plat de côtes* (ribs) are, however, sold on the bone. They are particularly tender and tasty, much like an *aiguillette baronne* (rump roast). You should braise beef for at least 2 hours. The *pot-au-feu,* the archetypical French boiled meat, should consist of an assortment of cuts, with and without bones, at the same time lean, soft, and gelatinous. All of the cuts suitable for braising will work. Moreover, it should include the *collier* (a cut from the neck), boned, and *plat de côtes couvert* (ribs), on the bone; these are indispensable to a *pot-au-feu. Poitrine* and *tendron* (both cuts from the brisket) are another welcome addition. And don't forget the *gîte-gîte* (shank) for its marrow bone or the *queue de boeuf* (oxtail), cut in pieces, for a variation on *pot-au-feu* called *hochepot.* Another classic is *boeuf gros sel*, which combines boiled beef with vegetables and an accompanying dish of coarse salt. However, for *boeuf à la ficelle* ("beef on a string"), which is served pink, use *romsteck*. To conclude, a word about the *paleron*, the part of the chuck located between the shoulder and body of the animal. It is perfect for *boeuf à la mode* (pot roast), but if it happens to come from a first-class animal, the butcher can turn it into a regular roast or cut it into pieces for a *fondue bourguignonne*.

A PERSPECTIVE ON BEEF

If you can talk beef with your butcher with competence as well as a smile, he will allow himself to be softened up and will always look after your needs.

It was the Egyptian civilization that transformed the role of sacrificial butcher into a profession. The Romans, great aficionados of meat, organized a powerful guild.

In antiquity, cattle were not cooked much; rather, they were sacrificed to the gods at the spring equinox, which at that time probably took place when the sun entered the constellation of Taurus. This custom, which goes back to the Egyptians, gave birth to the parade, no longer religious but now of a carnival nature, of *Boeuf gras*.

Here is what Alexandre Dumas wrote in his *Grande Dictionnaire de cuisine*, in 1873 (it was edited by Anatole France, who was working at the publisher A. Lemerre at the time):

> Beefsteak, or *bifteck à l'anglaise*. I remember seeing, after the campaign of 1815, when the English stayed two or three years in Paris, the birth of the steak in France . . . This did not occur, however, without a certain suspicion that the steak had been surreptitiously introduced into our midst. Nevertheless, since we are an eclectic nation and without prejudice, as soon as we realized that although the Greeks had arrived, the gift was not poisoned, we held out our plates and gave the steak its certificate of citizenship. Still, there are always several things that distinguish the English steak from the French steak. We make our steak with a slice of the loin, whereas our neighbors, for their beefsteaks, use a cut we call the *sous-noix de boeuf*, which

is to say the rump steak. There, however, this particular cut is always more tender than it is here, because they feed their cattle better and slaughter them younger than we do in France. So they take this part of beef and cut it into half-inch slices, flatten them a little, and cook them on a specially made cast-iron grill over coal rather than charcoal.

APHRODISIAC STEAK

◆ ◆ ◆

Le bifteck aphrodisiaque

"The man who has eaten this steak is capable of burying Hercules twelve times in the twelve hours that follow . . ."

Serves 4

1 teaspoon black peppercorns
½ teaspoon green peppercorns
½ teaspoon pink peppercorns
½ teaspoon juniper berries
½ teaspoon coriander seeds
Large pinch of Cayenne pepper
½ teaspoon cloves

1 teaspoon chopped fresh ginger
2 tablespoons pine nuts
4 steaks cut from the filet mignon (tenderloin), each about 6 ounces and about 1½ inches thick
Salt
1 tablespoon butter
¼ cup Cognac
1½ cups heavy cream

Combine the spices and pine nuts and, with a mortar and pestle or in a coffee grinder, grind coarsely. Coat the steaks with this mixture and season with salt to taste.

Heat a heavy skillet over moderately high heat. Add the butter and the steaks. Cook about 3 minutes per side for rare, about 4 minutes per side for medium rare. Remove the steaks from the pan. Deglaze the pan by adding the Cognac. Add the cream and boil until it is reduced by half.

Pour the sauce over the steaks and serve with green vegetables or a vegetable puree.

Wine: One of the spicy reds from the Rhône Valley, or even a Spanish red

SKIRT STEAK À LA BEAUJOLAISE

◆ ◆ ◆

Côtes de boeuf à la beaujolaise

Serves 4

2-pound skirt steak or	1 large celery stalk
London broil	Chervil
Salt	Parsley
1½ tablespoons oil	Chives
12 tablespoons butter	15 peppercorns
Ground black pepper	¾ cup Beaujolais
6 shallots	¼ cup aged red wine vinegar

Set a large heavy skillet over moderate heat. Lightly salt the meat on both sides. Add the oil and 1 tablespoon of the butter to the pan. When the butter is sizzling, add the meat and cook for 6 to 8 minutes on the first side. Turn it over and cook for an additional 6 to 8 minutes. Season the beef with pepper once it is browned. (It should be rare or medium rare.)

Chop the shallots and celery fine. Chop the chervil, parsley, and chives so that you have about 2 tablespoons of the herbs in all. Crush the peppercorns.

Remove the meat from the pan and keep warm. Pour off any fat from the pan, add a tablespoon butter, the shallots, and the celery and sauté briefly. Add the wine and vinegar and boil to reduce to a quarter. Remove the pan from the heat and add the remaining butter, bit by bit, stirring continuously, until it is fully incorporated. Add the chopped herbs and correct the seasoning.

Slice the meat across the grain in very thin slices. Serve the sauce on the side.

◆◆◆◆◆◆◆◆◆◆◆◆◆◆◆◆◆◆◆◆◆◆◆◆◆◆◆◆◆◆◆◆◆◆◆◆

DISCOUNTED
BEEF

◆ ◆ ◆

January and February
are difficult months for the pocketbook.
What better reason
to cook like the "poor."

◆◆◆

cooked
(leftover meat

La desserte is an elegant term from the *cuisine classique* designating leftover cooked meat, poultry, or fish that can be reused for other recipes, under various guises. The word *desserte* also refers to a small sideboard where dishes are placed once they have been removed from the table.

The *assiette anglaise* (an arrangement of several cold cooked meats) is the simplest and easiest way of reusing cooked meats. The *desserte* can be used to prepare cold dishes—composed salads, beef or fish salads, mousse for canapés, etc.—or hot dishes—*Hachis Parmentier* (see page 306), stuffings, *boeuf miroton* (beef with onion sauce), croquettes, and so on.

POT-AU-FEU SALAD

◆ ◆ ◆

Salade de pot-au-feu

See the previous chapter, under "Moving On to the Roast," for pot-au-feu.

Serves 4

1½ pounds boiled beef
6 small potatoes
Salt and pepper
1 onion plus chopped onion
  or shallot

Chopped parsley
⅓ cup dry white wine
1 tablespoon peanut oil
3 or 4 tomatoes

VINAIGRETTE

3 tablespoons wine vinegar
2 tablespoons mustard
⅓ cup olive oil

Chervil
Parsley
Chives

Cut the boiled beef across the grain into ¼-inch slices. Boil the potatoes, cut them in slices, and season with salt and pepper while they are still warm. Add a little chopped onion or shallot and a little chopped parsley. Add the wine and oil and toss. Toss from time to time.

Cut the tomatoes in thin slices. Slice an onion fine. Make the vinaigrette by stirring together the vinegar and mustard and slowly incorporating the oil. Add about a teaspoon total of the finely chopped herbs. Toss the beef with about half of this vinaigrette.

To serve, arrange the potatoes in the center of a serving platter or individual plates. Place the beef and tomatoes around the potatoes, top with the sliced onion, and sprinkle with the remaining vinaigrette.

VARIATION: You can also add the vegetables from a *pot-au-feu*, sliced and tossed with a vinaigrette. For this, combine 2 teaspoons dry mustard, salt and pepper, 3 tablespoons good vinegar, 7–8 tablespoons olive oil, a little chopped chervil and tarragon, and a chopped hard-boiled egg. Stir this together with a fork and toss with the beef and vegetables. Allow to marinate 1 hour before serving.

Boiled beef that is set aside to be served at another time should be placed on a plate and allowed to cool. Never let it chill in the cooking liquid.

Wine: Gamay de Touraine

BOILED BEEF LYONNAISE

◆ ◆ ◆

Boeuf bouilli à la lyonnaise

Serves 4

2 large onions
1½ tablespoons butter
1½ pounds boiled beef
Salt and pepper

1 tablespoon wine vinegar
2 tablespoons chopped
    parsley

Slice the onions. Heat the butter over moderate heat, add the onions, and sauté until golden. Slice the beef, add to the onions, and heat until it is cooked through. Season with salt and pepper. Add the vinegar, sprinkle with the parsley, and serve.

Wine: Beaujolais

BEEF À LA DIABLE

◆ ◆ ◆

Boeuf à la diable

Serves 4

4 thick slices of roast beef, 1½ cups bread crumbs
  each about 6 ounces ⅔ cup melted butter
7 tablespoons Dijon mustard

Brush each slice of beef with the mustard, then dip in the bread crumbs and finally in the butter. Broil briefly on both sides, or pan-fry it until the bread crumbs are golden. Serve with a Béarnaise sauce (see Appendix) to which you can add a few drops of Worcestershire or Tabasco sauce or with *Maître d'Hôtel* Butter (see Appendix) or with the vinaigrette used for the *Pot-au-feu* Salad (see page 92).

Wine: Crozes-Hermitage

BOILED BEEF
À LA POULETTE

◆ ◆ ◆

Boeuf bouilli à la poulette

Veal, chicken, and even fish can also be prepared this way.

Serves 4

3 tablespoons butter 1½ cups heavy cream
2 cups sliced mushrooms 4 slices of cooked meat,
2 shallots, chopped   each about 6 ounces
2 tablespoons white wine 2 egg yolks
  vinegar Juice of 1 lemon
¼ cup dry white wine

Heat 1 tablespoon of the butter in a saucepan over moderately high heat. Add the mushrooms and shallots and sauté until the mushrooms stop giving off liquid. Add the vinegar and cook until it has almost entirely evaporated. Add the white wine and boil until it has reduced by half. Add the cream and boil to reduce by about two thirds.

Melt the remaining butter, brush the meat (or fish) with it, and reheat for about 5 minutes in the oven.

Stir together the egg yolks and lemon juice. Stir into the sauce, being careful not to let it come to a boil. Spoon the sauce over the meat (or fish). Serve with noodles, rice, a vegetable puree, or steamed spinach.

Wines: White Côtes-du-Rhône, white Saint-Joseph, Saint-Péray

CROQUETTES

◆ ◆ ◆

You can use all sorts of leftover meat for this recipe, or you could mix several different sorts. Alternately, you could also use leftover fish.

Serves 3 to 4

⅔ cup rice
2 medium-sized onions
2 tablespoons butter
2 tablespoons broth or pan
  drippings
1 pound cooked meat,
  chopped
1 egg

1 tablespoon fresh thyme
  leaves
1 tablespoon chopped
  parsley
1 tablespoon chopped chives
Salt and pepper
Flour
1 tablespoon vegetable oil

Cook the rice in 1⅓ cups water until tender. Chop the onions and sauté in 1 tablespoon butter until soft. Add the broth. Stir together the rice, onions, chopped meat, egg, thyme, parsley, and chives. Season with salt and pepper.

Sprinkle a handful of flour over a plate. Using well-floured hands, form the mixture into balls the size of Ping-Pong balls. Roll in the flour.

Heat the remaining tablespoon butter with the oil in a large skillet over moderate heat. Fry the croquettes on all sides until golden. Blot on paper towels.

Serve with a salad or with a tomato sauce seasoned with basil and with spaghetti.

Wine: Chinon

A SACRED
FEAST

◆ ◆ ◆

*Easter and its traditions inaugurate
a cuisine of renewal.
The tender milk-fed lamb
offers itself up as the expiatory victim
to our gourmandise.
Whether spiced or stuffed,
it is the roast undergone metamorphosis.*

◆◆◆

Our Easter is intimately tied to food, but also to the moon. Its date is determined according to the first Saturday night after the first full moon of spring, which is to say the full moon that falls after the spring equinox of about March 21. This limits the holiday to the interval between March 22 and April 25.

In the Eastern Orthodox Church, traditions are similar, but much more scrupulously observed, and the famous red-painted Easter eggs are eaten with an egg-enriched braided loaf; while for the Jewish Passover the ritual demands unleavened bread. The paschal lamb, which figures in all our traditions, is milk-fed. Here, as a curiosity, is a medieval recipe: "Take a lamb and skin it as usual. Take out the entrails and wash the cavity well but do not remove the feet. Then take the lungs and liver and boil them along with the other entrails. Mix this preparation with parsley, bacon, other spices, raisins, and salt. Stuff the lamb and sew it tight. Place the lamb lengthwise on a spit and attach its feet in the manner of a hare's so that they do not move. This dish is suitable for nobility." (Some, for this holiday, replaced the stuffing simply with the entrails and herbs.)

Compare this to Roland Dorgelès's recipe for "lamb in the Kurdish style": "Take a small milk-fed lamb, one of the lambs that the nomadic shepherds carry like children. Draw it, season the cavity, and fill it with a seasoned stuffing made of its offal: the liver, lungs, and heart. Finish off the stuffing with partially cooked rice mixed with dry unsweetened apricots, which you have cooked in some juice. Truss the lamb and roast it. Serve it with the degreased cooking juices."

Since the cinnamon tree is the tree of the moon, here is a recipe worthy of our holiday.

LEG OF MILK-FED LAMB
WITH CINNAMON

◆ ◆ ◆

Gigot d'agneau de lait macéré
à la cannelle

The flavor of milk-fed lamb is halfway between those of veal and ordinary lamb. This lamb is available from specialized butchers, particularly in Greek communities, in the spring. You may be able to convince your butcher to order it for you.

Serves 4

2½–3-pound leg of milk-fed
   lamb
8 tablespoons cinnamon
Salt and pepper
⅓ cup vegetable oil
1 large onion

3 tablespoons butter
1⅓ cups rice
½ cup raisins
2 tablespoons slivered
   almonds (optional)

Sprinkle the leg of lamb all over with 6 tablespoons of the cinnamon. Cover, refrigerate, and allow to marinate for 6 hours. Season with salt and pepper.

Preheat the oven to 375° F.

Heat the oil over moderately high heat in a roasting pan or flameproof casserole large enough to hold the lamb. Add the meat and sear on all sides until lightly browned. Set in the oven and cook, uncovered, for about 25 minutes. To judge doneness, you can pierce it with a sharp knife; the juices should still be very pink.

In the meantime, chop the onion fine. In a flameproof casserole, heat 2 tablespoons of the butter and sauté the onion until soft. Add the rice, the remaining 2 tablespoons cinnamon, and the raisins and mix well. Season with salt and pepper. Add 2 cups water, bring to a boil, cover, and bake in the preheated oven for about 20 minutes. When the rice is cooked, fluff it with a fork and stir in the remaining 1 tablespoon butter. You could also add 2 tablespoons of slivered almonds.

Carve the lamb and serve with the rice.

Wine: Côte-Rôtie

SPICED MILK-FED LAMB

◆ ◆ ◆

Agneau de lait épicé

See the note about milk-fed lamb in the preceding recipe. Five-spice powder is available in Asian groceries and some supermarkets.

Serves 4

2 pounds boneless shoulder of milk-fed lamb
2 tablespoons curry powder
2 teaspoons powdered cardamom
½ teaspoon cinnamon
½ teaspoon five-spice powder
⅓ cup vegetable oil

2 large onions, sliced
2 cloves garlic, chopped
1½ teaspoons chopped fresh ginger
4 large tomatoes, peeled, seeded, and chopped
10 mint leaves, chopped
1¼ cups dry white wine
Salt

FOR THE RICE

2 tablespoons butter
1 large onion, finely
  chopped
1⅓ cups rice
½ teaspoon chopped fresh
  ginger

½ teaspoon *quatre-épices* (*see
  note on page 54*)
½ cup raisins
Salt

Cut the lamb shoulder into 1½-inch pieces. Season with the curry, cardamom, cinnamon, and five-spice powder. Heat the oil in a large flameproof casserole over moderately high heat. Add the meat and brown. Add the onions, garlic, and ginger. Stir well to combine. Add the tomatoes, mint, wine, 1¼ cups water, and salt to taste. Bring to a boil. Cover and simmer for about 1 hour, until the lamb is tender. Alternately, bake in a preheated 325° F. oven.

For the rice, heat the butter in a saucepan over moderate heat. Add the onion and sauté until soft. Add the rice, ginger, *quatre-épices*, raisins, and salt to taste, and mix well. Add 2 cups water, bring to a boil, cover, and bake in a preheated 325° F. oven for about 20 minutes. When the rice is cooked, fluff it with a fork.

Serve the lamb with the rice on the side.

Wine: Bandol

LAMB ON A
BENDER

◆ ◆ ◆

When a simple "country wine" encounters
a flavorsome morsel,
a happy marriage may well result.
A sip of Bandol and a taste of lamb with white beans
will transport you directly to the sun-drenched
slopes of Provence.

◆◆◆

Even while the Côtes-de-Provence, the Coteaux-d'Aix, and Coteaux-des-Baux-en-Provence let themselves be seduced by grape varietals—such as Cabernet Sauvignon—that are supposed to "embellish" their wines, preferring to give up their typical character in the hopes of wider appeal, the little vineyard of Bandol remains loyal to its local varietal, the *mourvèdre*, a grape that insists nevertheless on continuing to be difficult and demanding. We can be thankful to the wine makers who, in order to improve their wines, have given up the PLC (a waiver under France's strict *Appellation d'Origine Contrôlée* [AOC] system, which allows a vineyard to produce additional grapes, generally about 20 percent more than the mandated quantity base). Thus Bandol can assert its generous personality and emerge from the anonymous crowd. Growing in dry soil, high in silicon and calcium, the *mourvèdre* makes a wine redolent of pepper, spice, and musk, and at times tobacco. It can be unyielding in its youth. It is balanced by the addition of Grenache, a more seductive varietal that tastes of licorice, dried fruit, and plums. You should never drink a real Bandol until it is at least five years old: thus it is a wine that is best cellared. This appellation also produces whites and rosés. The wine goes well with a _daube_ (a slow-cooked stew or braise), a _civet_ (a very rich stew) made with wild rabbit or game, and also with roasts as long as they are well aged. I have relished a Bandol, Domaine Tempier, 1984, along with a leg of lamb with fresh white beans and onions (_gigot d'agneau aux haricots blancs frais et aux oignons_).

Gigot (leg of lamb) takes its name from an ancient musical instrument, the _gigue_, which resembles it in shape. The French, being the meat eaters they are, are avid consumers of first pork, then beef, but topping the hit parade of classic cuisine is leg of lamb with flageolets. A longtime symbol of Parisian butchers, this choice cut was "awaited like a Sunday love tryst by bourgeois gourmands."

Victor Hugo fortified himself by devouring an entire leg of lamb at a time, while Emile Zola may be the author who has most often cited this cut. With regard to the beans, we can thank Catherine de Médicis for introducing them to France. Engaged to the Dauphin, she was packing her trunks before she sailed for Marseilles in 1533 when she received a bag of beans from the Canon Valeriano as a wedding present. Pope Clement VII had been the first to obtain them from the New World.

LEG OF LAMB WITH
WHITE BEANS AND ONIONS

◆ ◆ ◆

Gigot d'agneau aux haricots blancs frais
et aux oignons

You will note that the ingredients list 18 large onions. This is not a typographical error. As they cook, the onions become very soft and sweet, adding a remarkable silkiness to the beans. If you cannot find fresh beans, by all means use dried. Simply substitute 2 pounds dried beans and soak them overnight before using.

Serves 8 to 10

18 large onions
4 carrots
1 small head celery
4 large tomatoes (or 2 cups canned plum tomatoes)
4 bay leaves
1 small bunch of fresh thyme
4½ pounds fresh white beans *or dried*

⅓ cup peanut oil
6–7-pound leg of lamb, boned and tied
Salt and pepper
⅔ cup butter
4 garlic cloves, crushed
3 tablespoons chopped chives

Slice fine 2 of the onions, the carrots, celery, and tomatoes. Combine in a large flameproof casserole with 12 cups water, the bay leaves, and half the thyme. Bring to a boil and then simmer 20 minutes. Strain. Combine this vegetable broth with the beans and cook about 1 hour 15 minutes, until the beans are tender.

Preheat the oven to 350° F.

Slice the remaining 16 onions. Set a large roasting pan over moderately high heat. Add the oil. Season the leg of lamb with salt and pepper. Brown well in the oil. Remove the lamb and sprinkle with the remaining thyme. Reduce the heat to moderate. Add the butter, onions, and garlic, season with salt, and sauté until softened. Set the lamb on top of the onions and roast in the preheated oven about 1 hour 15 minutes for rare meat. Stir the onions frequently so that they do not burn. Remove the lamb and set on a rack for 45 minutes over a pan so that the juices that drip down can be saved.

When the beans are cooked, there should be little or no water left in the pan. Add the roast onions and lamb juices to the beans, season with salt and pepper, and let stew for 10 minutes. Reheat the lamb for 10 to 15 minutes in the oven. Stir the chives into the beans just before serving. Carve the lamb and serve with the beans.

When Bandol is wedded to the lamb, the wine seems exceptionally elegant. The encounter combines the delicate aromas of thyme and bay leaf with the pepper and cinnamon notes emanating from the wine. It is an almost complete expression of the harsh yet beautiful Mediterranean landscape.

GASCONNADE

◆ ◆ ◆

This is an old recipe from the Pyrenees and was traditionally roasted on a spit in front of a hot fire with the juices dripping into a pan set below the lamb. The following is a slightly tamer adaptation.

Serves 8 to 10

1 pound garlic	Salt and pepper
10 anchovy fillets	1 cup lamb or beef broth
6–7-pound leg of lamb	

Preheat the oven to 450° F.

Peel 6 large garlic cloves and cut each lengthwise into 5 slivers. Cut each anchovy fillet in 3. Using a small sharp knife, make slits in the lamb and insert a sliver of garlic and anchovy in each, making sure none of the garlic sticks out. Do this all over the leg at evenly spaced intervals. Rub all over with salt and pepper.

Set the lamb on a rack in a roasting pan and roast about 1½ hours, depending on desired doneness.

In the meantime, separate the remaining garlic into cloves without peeling. Bring a large pan of water to a boil. Add the garlic and boil about 5 minutes. Drain and cool the garlic under cold running water. Peel.

When the lamb is cooked, remove it from the oven and let it sit 10 minutes. Pour off the fat from the pan, add the broth and garlic cloves, and simmer for 5 minutes, scraping the bottom of the pan. Carve the lamb and serve with the garlic sauce.

The best wine to serve is a red Irouleguy, AOC-produced in the southwest, in the department of Pyrénées-Atlantiques. The vineyards cover about 225 acres in the Basque mountains. The grapes that go into the red (Cabernet Franc, Cabernet Sauvignon, and Tannat) give us a tannic wine perfumed with scents reminiscent of ripe fruit and venison.

PHARAOH'S PULLET

◆ ◆ ◆

Its genus is called Numida,
evoking Africa, its land of origin.
In French it is called pintade,
from the Portuguese pintada, *meaning "speckled."*
What is it?
The guinea fowl, a winged comestible
which is now acclimated the world over.

◆◆◆◆◆◆◆◆◆◆◆◆◆◆◆◆◆◆◆◆◆◆◆◆◆◆◆◆◆◆◆◆◆◆◆◆◆◆◆

There are guinea fowl depicted on frescoes in the tombs that go back almost forty centuries. At that time, the Egyptians already knew how to incubate the eggs artificially: on clay bricks heated by burning camel dung. It seems that they were quite successful at it, since nearly 70 percent hatched, at times producing up to 90,000 eggs. But what did they do to maintain the appropriate temperature? It was a family secret, they say, and jealously guarded. Around the year 400 B.C., the fowl show up again, this time in Greek mythology. This is where we get the species name *meleagris*. Atropos, one of the three Fates, decided that Meleager, the king of Calydon, would survive only as long as a brand that was burning in the entrance hall at the moment of his birth. His mother, Althea, was shrewd enough to preserve the brand by extinguishing it. However, in the course of a brawl, Meleager killed his uncles, and in order to kill him, his mother threw the brand on the fire. His sister so mourned for him that they died of sorrow. Out of compassion, Artemis retrieved them from Hades and turned them into guinea hens. Their tears became the white pearls that decorate the plumage of these birds. This is the story Ovid tells in his *Metamorphoses*.

In Rome, the guinea fowl was known as hen of Carthage, of Numidia, or of the pharaoh, which is where its Italian name, *faraona*, comes from. Rabelais, for his part, speaks of the *guynette*. It may well have been the Portuguese who introduced it to Europe from Africa (from Guinea?). The bird does not appear under the name *pintade* until about 1643. Confusion arises because the French also called it *poule de Turquie* ("Turkish hen"), as well as *poule d'Inde* ("Indian hen").

Guinea fowl are seldom cited in ancient cookbooks. I did find this anecdote, recounted by André Castelot, citing Courchamp (1783–1849), a French writer on gastronomy. The Abbé de Matignon, Bishop of Lisieux and a great fancier of guinea fowl, was well known for his humorous ways.

"Why do you not sell my guinea fowl for four *pistoles* apiece, as you do the parrots, which are half their size?" he said to his farmer.

"That's because the guineas will not speak a word to Monseigneur," the peasant replied.

"Just because my guineas don't speak doesn't mean they don't think," the abbé superbly replied.

GUINEA HEN WITH WATERCRESS

◆ ◆ ◆

Pintade cressonnière

Serves 4

6 medium-sized onions	1½ tablespoons aged red
9 tablespoons butter	wine vinegar
2 guinea hens	Salt and pepper
4 slices of bacon	3 bunches of watercress
Vegetable oil	(about 4 cups tightly
1 pimiento	packed)
¼ pound slab bacon, cut	2 cups heavy cream
into ¼-inch dice	1 teaspoon pink peppercorns
½ pound *mâche*	

Preheat the oven to 400° F.

Peel the onions and cut into thin rings. Melt 8 tablespoons of the butter in a roasting pan over moderate heat, add the onions, and sauté until they are soft. Truss the guinea hens and lay 2 slices bacon over the breast of each. Place breast side up on the bed of onions and set in the preheated oven. Roast for 25 to 35 minutes, until the breasts are cooked but still pink. Baste with a little oil from time to time and stir the onions occasionally so that they do not burn.

Cut the pimiento into 8 thin strips. Heat and keep warm.

Carve the guinea hen breasts and keep warm, covered with foil. Return the legs to the oven with the onions for another 20 minutes. If the onions are browning too quickly, add a little water to keep them from burning.

Set the diced slab bacon in a small saucepan, cover with cold water, bring to a boil, and continue to boil for 1 minute. Drain and cool under cold running water. Cut off the roots of the mâche and wash thoroughly. Heat the remaining 1 table-spoon butter in a skillet, add the bacon, and fry until the bacon just begins to brown. Add the mâche and let wilt for a few seconds. Season with 1 tablespoon of the vinegar and salt and pepper. Keep warm.

To prepare the sauce, remove the leaves from the watercress. Wash and drain well. Pour the cream into a wide-bottomed non-reactive saucepan over moderate heat and boil to reduce to about 1⅓ cups. Add the watercress leaves and cook 3 min-utes. Pour into a blender and puree to make a green sauce. Add the remaining ½ tablespoon vinegar and season with salt and pepper.

To serve, use the pimiento strips to make 2 circles at the top of each plate. Spoon a little mâche in the middle of each. At the bottom of each plate, set a mound of onions with the carved breast on top. Place a leg in the center of each plate and top with the green sauce. Sprinkle a little coarsely crushed pink peppercorn on each side. Serve hot.

Wine: A well-aged red Chinon

THE AGILE
RABBIT

◆ ◆ ◆

The story of this prolific lagomorph
begins in Africa.
It was introduced to France
in the Middle Ages, via Spain.
After many changes in fortune,
it finally won a place of honor on our tables.

◆◆

Pliny and Varro report that Tarragona, in Spain, totally collapsed as a consequence of the rabbits that had dug their burrows underneath the houses of the city and that most of the inhabitants were buried in the ruins. I do not know if the authors meant this seriously. However, Strabo, too, recounts how the Balearic Islanders appealed to Rome to help destroy the rabbits, which were reproducing there excessively. Another story comes to us from the Lipari Islands, where these lagomorphs were ravaging the harvest. The local farmers cleverly imported a considerable number of cats.

Rabbits were to become an even greater nuisance in Australia, where they were introduced at the end of the nineteenth century. Subsequently, 25 million had to be killed in 1907, and then several hundred million more in 1925.

In France, Louis XVI, in his war against rabbits, declared them vermin and allowed everyone to hunt them. In 1950, a veterinarian, exasperated by seeing his property ransacked, inoculated several specimens with myxomatosis. Three years later, the rabbit population was almost completely wiped out, and hunting rabbits was prohibited for several years. But the population recovered very quickly, thanks to its rapid birth rate.

RABBIT ISIDORIA

◆ ◆ ◆

Lapin Isidoria

Serves 4

3½–4-pound rabbit	¼ pound shredded cabbage
5 tablespoons butter	(about 3 cups)
4 onions	2 garlic cloves
¼ pound slab bacon	1 tablespoon mustard
2 shallots	1 cup shelled fresh fava
1 tablespoon chopped chives	beans
Salt and pepper	4 slices of peasant-style
16 large spinach leaves	French or Italian bread

Cut (or have your butcher cut) both the front and the hind legs off the rabbit. Bone the loins by running a sharp knife along each side of the backbone, then carefully cutting along the rib cage. Reserve the kidneys and liver separately.

Preheat the oven to 300° F.

Heat 2 tablespoons of the butter in a large ovenproof casserole over moderately high heat. Add the rabbit legs and brown on all sides. Remove and set aside. Slice 2 of the onions fine, add to the casserole, and cook until soft. Place the legs on the onions, set in the oven, and cook about 45 minutes, or until the meat is cooked through. Debone the hind legs and shred the meat. Reserve the front legs; separately, reserve the bones and onions. Dice the bacon and sauté until lightly browned. Pour off all but 1 tablespoon of the fat. Add the shallots and cook until softened, then add the shredded rabbit meat and chives. Season with salt and pepper. Heat 1 tablespoon of the butter in a skillet, add the spinach, and cook, turning it frequently, until it is just barely wilted. Line 4 (4-inch) ramekins with the spinach leaves and fill with the rabbit mixture, pressing it down as much as possible.

Heat 1 tablespoon of the butter over moderate heat, add the cabbage, stir, cover, and cook until the cabbage is tender.

Using a heavy chef's knife or cleaver, cut up the rabbit bones. Coarsely chop the 2 remaining onions and combine with the bones and garlic in a saucepan. Cover with 2 cups of water, bring to a steady simmer, and cook to reduce by half. Strain and season with salt and pepper. Stir in the onions you had cooked with the rabbit legs and continue to simmer until slightly thickened.

Increase the oven temperature to 400° F.

Rub the rabbit loins with a little salt and pepper and brush with the mustard. Roast in the hot oven for about 12 minutes, or until just pink at the center.

Set the ramekins in a small roasting pan, fill the roasting pan with enough boiling water to come halfway up the sides of the ramekins, and place the pan in the oven for about 5 minutes, or until the rabbit mixture is heated through.

Boil the fava beans for 5 to 8 minutes in salted water until tender. In a food processor, coarsely puree the fava beans. Season. Cut the bread in triangles and toast. Spread the puree on the toast.

Heat the remaining 1 tablespoon butter over moderately high heat, add the rabbit kidneys and liver, and brown. Both should be a little pink when cooked. Season with salt and pepper.

To serve, place half a front leg at the top of each plate; set a kidney or piece of liver on one side and the toast triangles with fava puree on the other. Unmold a ramekin in the center; then arrange the cabbage on one side. Slice the loin and place on the other side. Moisten with the reduced rabbit and onion broth.

Wine: An aged Chinon

RABBIT WITH SAGE

◆ ◆ ◆

Lapin à l'infusion de sauge

Caul fat is often used in sausage making and is available from better butchers.

Serves 4

3½–4-pound rabbit
Salt and pepper
¾ pound caul fat
20 large sage leaves
4 ripe tomatoes
3 tablespoons white wine
   vinegar

2 cups heavy cream
¾ pound fresh fettuccine
½ teaspoon chopped fresh
   herbs (one or more of
   parsley, chervil, and
   chives)

Preheat the oven to 450° F.

Cut the rabbit into 8 pieces, season with salt and pepper, and carefully wrap each piece in the caul fat.

Bring ¾ cup water to a boil, add the sage leaves, remove from the heat, and infuse for 20 minutes. Strain.

Roast the rabbit for 20 to 30 minutes in the preheated oven. Peel and seed the tomatoes, then dice.

Remove the rabbit from the roasting pan, remove and discard the caul fat, and keep the rabbit warm. Pour off the fat from the pan and set over moderately high heat. Add the vinegar and boil until it has almost completely evaporated. Add the sage infusion and reduce by three quarters. Add the cream and boil to reduce by half. Season with salt and pepper.

Boil the fettuccine until it is cooked through, about 5 minutes. Drain and toss with ¼ cup of the sauce, the tomatoes, and the chopped herbs.

Serve the rabbit with the pasta and the remaining sauce.

Wine: White Châteauneuf-du-Pape

ROAST RABBIT WITH MUSTARD

◆ ◆ ◆

Lapin rôti à la moutarde

Serves 4

3½–4-pound rabbit
3 tablespoons strong Dijon
   mustard

½ pound caul fat (see
   preceding recipe)
2 large sprigs of fresh thyme

Preheat the oven to 375° F.

Brush the rabbit inside and out with mustard, set it on the caul fat, and wrap the rabbit carefully in it.

Set the wrapped rabbit on a roasting rack in a roasting pan, sprinkle generously with thyme leaves, and roast for 40 to 45 minutes. Remove the fat.

If you wish to have a sauce, sprinkle the rabbit with 3 tablespoons vegetable oil before cooking. When it is cooked, pour off the fat, add 2 tablespoons of *crème fraîche* to the pan juices, strain, and season with salt and pepper.

Serve with rice or with pasta in a basil-accented tomato sauce.

Wine: Crozes-Hermitage, Morey-Saint-Denis

FOIE GRAS
DELIVERED

◆ ◆ ◆

Foie gras, whether it comes
from geese or from ducks,
through its aromatic finesse
and its sensual density seems a concentrate of all
the goodness of the earth.
Eyes brighten and every palate is primed
in the presence of this gastronomic jewel.

◆◆◆◆◆◆◆◆◆◆◆◆◆◆◆◆◆◆◆◆◆◆◆◆◆◆◆◆◆◆◆◆◆◆◆◆◆◆◆

L et's begin by clarifying some distinctions. The flavor of goose foie gras is all nuance. The fattened liver is soft to the touch, creamy, and satiny, with the scent of goose fat. It is generally sweeter and perhaps a little more civilized than duck foie gras. The latter is more plump, darker, and redolent of duck. Generally, it is also more bitter. Liver contains elements that are sour, sweet, and bitter; it is the hand of man that brings in the fourth flavor, salt.

The character of a liver will vary according to its origin and the manner in which the bird was force-fed. This is why we have asked the *chambre syndicale de la haute cuisine française* (the Chamber of Commerce devoted to furthering the culinary arts) to require this information on all foie gras.

In general, goose foie gras is better cold than hot; however, don't serve it too cold. Duck liver can be prepared both ways. A good liver should be firm without being hard or brittle, otherwise it will shrink too much and be granular when cooked. It ought to be glossy and pink or a little yellow—if it has been fed with corn—but never a dark or reddish gray. Avoid liver that is bruised or blemished. Some people soak it in ice water or milk for 2 hours to mellow the flavor. If you do, make sure you dry it well afterward.

If you buy it preserved, avoid buying foie gras labeled *"conserve,"* since it is usually overcooked, and opt for *"semi-conserve,"* or partially cooked.

RAW OR COOKED

You can eat raw foie gras, thinly sliced, on perfectly toasted country bread. Add freshly ground white pepper and coarse salt and drink a Pacherenc-du-Vic-Bilh, a mellow wine from Béarn.

Sautéed slices of foie gras are just as easy to cook as calf's liver. Cut ¼-inch slices a little on the bias. Lightly dip in flour and season with a little salt. Place them in a hot frying pan and turn them when the first pink drop appears. Cook the same way on the other side. Blot on a paper towel and season with pepper. You can deglaze the pan by pouring in a little wine vinegar. Add kernels of fresh corn to the pan and a little Jurançon or Sauternes.

Serve the liver on warm plates with the sauce on top.

FOIE GRAS TERRINE
WITH BANYULS

◆ ◆ ◆

Terrine de foie gras de canard au banyuls

Prepare the terrine 3 or 4 days before you plan to serve it. You will find that the foie gras available in the United States is already partly cleaned; thus there is likely to be no green where the gall came in contact with the liver, and few blood particles. You will, however, need to devein it. This is done mainly for aesthetic reasons, so it is better to err on the side of caution and remove too few veins rather than too many. You want to keep

*the livers as intact as possible. You can check for doneness when cooking
by inserting an instant-reading meat thermometer into the center of the liver;
it should read 110° F.*

Serves 6 to 8

1 ¼ pounds duck foie gras
½ teaspoon salt
¼ teaspoon white pepper
Pinch of sugar

2 tablespoons duck or goose
fat
3 ½ tablespoons Banyuls (*see
Glossary of Wines and Spirits*)

One or 2 hours before you begin, remove the liver from the
refrigerator and allow it to warm to room temperature. With
the help of a knife, remove the fine skin that covers the liver
and also the greenish part that may have come in contact with
the gall. Separate the 2 parts; one lobe will be larger than the
other.

Set the larger part, smooth side down, on a cutting board.
Make an incision in the liver, down the center, starting about
½ inch from either end and about ¾ inch deep. Open up the
incision and use your fingers to loosen the large white vein.
Carefully remove it, along with the smaller veins. Also remove
the small bits of blood that you may find. Repeat this operation
with the smaller lobe.

Preheat the oven to 250° F.

Season the liver on all sides with the salt, pepper, and sugar.
Place the larger lobe in an earthenware terrine in such a way
that it conforms to the shape of the container. Add the other
lobe and press down so that they fill the terrine.

Melt the duck fat and combine with the Banyuls and 3 ½
tablespoons water. Pour this mixture into the terrine. Set the
terrine in a larger pan. Fill this pan with boiling water so that
the water comes about halfway up the terrine. Place in the
oven and cook, uncovered, for about 25 minutes. Test for
doneness by inserting a metal skewer in the center of the

terrine: if it is warm, the terrine is done. Let cool. Wrap tightly and refrigerate.

Serve with toasted peasant bread and Banyuls.

So what is the best wine with foie gras? If you decide to go with a Sauternes, it should be at least 10 years old, because if it's too young it doesn't provide sufficient complexity. Certainly, goose foie gras with a well-aged Sauternes is sensational. You should, however, avoid duck foie gras with the wine.

If you prefer Champagne, you will require a quality vintage bottle such as a Gosset, Krug, or Bollinger RD.

Another possibility is a mellow Jurançon. It pairs more happily with duck foie gras than with goose. Alsatian wines, once again of a good vintage, are better with goose liver.

Should you decide on red wine, it will have to be at least 5 or 6 years old, a little tannic and unctuous. This combination is difficult to achieve, but if you should find it, the interplay of flavor will be exceptional, because of the structure of the wine. Volnay comes to mind.

Divert yourself, as you explore the possibilities, by taking notes. That way, you will avoid repeating errors and improve the likelihood of a better match.

HOLD YOUR
TONGUE

◆ ◆ ◆

While this may at times be fine advice,
to those who are fond of them,
tongues are also
a delicious object of gastronomy.
You can fully gratify your papillae
by tastefully preparing those of another.

◆◆◆◆◆◆◆◆◆◆◆◆◆◆◆◆◆◆◆◆◆◆◆◆◆◆◆◆◆◆◆◆◆◆◆◆◆◆

Now that mathematics and binary language have replaced the ancient tongues, it is difficult for a host to keep up
his part at the dinner table, seeing that it is his role to make
every guest feel at ease, by encouraging each to speak of himself. And what should we think, in fact, of someone aspiring
to the reputation of a gastronome who would remain frightfully
tongue-tied when conversation turns to beef, calf, lamb, or
pork tongues? Indeed, are there really living tongues lovelier
than these fine tongues, lovingly prepared, which have never
slandered, lied, or blasphemed?

Silence the excessively loquacious by serving them one of
these lovely dead tongues. They are certainly an excellent thing
to learn about, never monotonous; moreover, you can vary the
preparation a hundred ways. Furthermore, they are never tire-
some, never too spicy or salty in able hands. They make a
pleasing gift to everyone and are sufficiently wise never to
make enemies. These are the words of Grimod de La Reynière.

MY RECIPE FOR
CALF'S TONGUE

◆ ◆ ◆

Langue de veau à ma manière

Serves 4

1 calf's tongue
Salt
1 leek
2 onions
4 carrots
1 large sprig of thyme
1 bay leaf
1 tablespoon mustard
1 tablespoon lemon juice
1 tablespoon aged red wine
    vinegar
½ cup olive oil

⅓ cup peanut oil
2 tablespoons chopped
    chives
2 tablespoons chopped fresh
    tarragon
⅓ cup chopped parsley
Pepper
4 heads Boston lettuce
2 tablespoons butter
1 hard-boiled egg
Chervil leaves

Soak the calf's tongue for at least 4 hours or overnight in plenty of water in the refrigerator. Put the tongue in a large saucepan, cover with water, add a little salt, and bring to a boil. Drain the tongue and rinse. Put the tongue back in the pan. Slice and clean the leek, slice 1 of the onions and 2 of the carrots, and add to the pan along with the thyme and bay leaf. Cover with water, add a little salt, bring to a boil, then reduce the heat to a simmer and cook for about 1½ hours. The tongue is cooked when the skin can be easily removed and the flesh is tender. Remove the skin.

Stir together the mustard, lemon juice, and vinegar. Gradually add the oils, stirring continuously. Finally add the chopped herbs and season with salt and pepper.

Preheat the oven to 375° F.

Remove any wilted leaves from the lettuces. Bring a large

pan of water to a boil. Plunge the lettuces into the boiling water for about 3 minutes; drain. Chop the remaining carrots and onion fine. Melt the butter in a non-reactive, flameproof casserole on the stove, add the remaining carrots and onion, and sauté until soft. Place the lettuces on top of this mixture, add enough water so that it comes halfway up the lettuces, bring to a boil, then place, covered, in the oven and bake 40 minutes. Using a slotted spatula, remove the lettuces, drain, and arrange in the center of a serving platter. Slice the tongue and distribute it around the lettuce. Coarsely chop the egg and stir into the vinaigrette. Spoon over the tongue only. Decorate with chervil leaves.

Wine: White Saint-Joseph

BEEF TONGUE *EN TORTUE*

◆ ◆ ◆

Langue de boeuf en tortue

Chef Senderens recommends that you purchase your herbe à tortue *at the deluxe Parisian food shop Fauchon. Should this present difficulties, you can make your own herb mixture by combining equal parts of dried ground basil, thyme, bay leaf, and marjoram.*

Serves 4

1 beef tongue	Pepper
Salt	1 cup green olives
2 leeks	1 cup cornichons
4 onions	5 large ripe tomatoes
3 carrots	1 garlic clove
3 sprigs of thyme	1 chicken bouillon cube
3 bay leaves	1 tablespoon *herbe à tortue*
1 pound mushrooms	⅓ cup Port
2 tablespoons butter	

Soak the beef tongue for at least 4 hours or overnight in plenty of water in the refrigerator. Put the tongue in a large saucepan, cover with water, add a little salt, and bring to a boil. Drain the tongue and rinse. Put the tongue back in the pan. Slice and clean 1 of the leeks, slice 1 of the onions and 2 of the carrots, and add to the pan along with a sprig of thyme and a bay leaf. Cover with water, add a little salt, bring to a boil, then reduce the heat to a simmer and cook about 1½ hours. The tongue is cooked when the skin can be easily removed and the flesh is tender. Remove the skin.

Wash and slice the mushrooms. Heat 1 tablespoon of the butter in a skillet over moderately high heat, add the mushrooms, and cook until they stop giving off liquid. Season with salt and pepper. Pit the olives. Slice the cornichons lengthwise.

Slice 2 of the remaining onions. Peel the tomatoes, remove the seeds, and cut into quarters. Melt the remaining butter, add the onions, and sauté until soft. Add the tomatoes. Chop the garlic, and stir in along with a sprig of thyme and a bay leaf. Cover and cook at a bare simmer for 1 hour. Remove the bay leaf.

In another saucepan, combine the bouillon cube with 2 cups water. Chop the remaining carrot, onion, and leek and add to this broth, along with the remaining sprig of thyme and bay leaf. Bring to a boil and simmer 20 minutes. Remove from the heat, stir in the *herbe à tortue*, and allow it to infuse for 15 minutes. Strain and reserve this broth. Combine with the tomato sauce and Port. Boil this mixture to reduce by half until you have obtained an unctuous sauce. Add the mushrooms, olives, and cornichons. Taste for seasoning.

Slice the tongue and reheat in the sauce for 5 minutes. Serve the tongue accompanied by a rice pilaf if you wish.

Wine: Côte-Rôtie

HARE TODAY

◆ ◆ ◆

Get to know hare,
its gamy flavor and its "black" meat.
The male, or buck hare, is polygamous.
He will fight his adversaries
with fierce abandon
to possess a female.

◆◆

Depending on its age, hare is given different names in French. The *levraut* (2 to 4 months old, about 3 pounds) is best roasted; the *trois-quart* (7 to 8 months old, 6 to 7 pounds) is ideal for its saddle, which is usually roasted as well as used for sautés. As with a wild rabbit, you can recognize the animal's age by the softness of the ears and the delicacy of the paws. The young hare also has a small protuberance about the size of a lentil on the lower joint of the forepaw. This characteristic disappears as it ages. We prefer to use young hares in cooking, since they yield the best result. The *capucin* (more than a year old, 9 to 13 pounds) is mostly made into a stew or *civet*, *daube*, terrine, or pâté. Its fur will be dull, its teeth beginning to yellow, its claws long, and its snout flattened.

Carefully examine the hare you are about to buy, since the shot may have caused wounds that will make it difficult to prepare and sometimes inedible. This is game that goes bad quickly. It should be consumed without hanging or aging. Joseph Favre, who wrote the most famous culinary dictionary that I know of (*Dictionnaire universel de cuisine et hygiène alimentaire*, published in the late nineteenth century), said: "The formulas that may be applied to cooking hare are numerous, and some of them should never have seen the light of day." He later adds: "You must never stray from the principle that a hare roasted on the spit (or in the oven) without marinating must be very fresh, this being the only condition under which it can be cooked rare. On the other hand, hare that is not strictly fresh must be marinated and the cooking time should be doubled. It therefore has to be braised, since the meat will be too dry once it is cooked past the pink stage."

Be careful how your hare is butchered, as if this is not done attentively, the bones will splinter. It is best to cut the bones through the joints. Hare is served with chestnut puree or with whole chestnuts, which should always be cooked with a celery rib, or with a gratin of celery root (with potatoes), and, of course, with gooseberry or bilberry (*myrtille*) jelly or with unsweetened apple butter. Pears also go well with hare. Finally, try a spiced sweet potato puree made by caramelizing a little sugar in butter, adding the peeled, diced sweet potatoes, and cooking until they fall apart. Then puree and add ginger, nutmeg, and cloves to taste. It's a real treat.

HARE ROASTED ON A SPIT

◆ ◆ ◆

Lièvre à la broche

Serves 5

1 young hare
Salt and pepper
3 large sprigs of thyme
¼ teaspoon lavender
1 bay leaf
¼ teaspoon ground juniper
¼ teaspoon ground cumin
1 tablespoon Dijon mustard
1 tablespoon chopped
    shallots

3 tablespoons butter, plus
    more for sautéing
    (optional)
3 tablespoons aged red wine
    vinegar
1 cup heavy cream
¾ pound fresh fettuccine

Season the hare with salt and pepper. Rub the cavity with 2 of the sprigs of thyme, lavender, crushed bay leaf, juniper, and cumin. Brush with the mustard. Roast for 30 to 40 minutes on a spit in front of a fire with a roasting pan beneath to catch the juices. If you can, add vine and juniper cuttings to the fire. Alternately, preheat an oven to 450° F., set the hare on a roasting rack in a roasting pan, and roast for 30 to 40 minutes, until the hare is cooked but still pink inside. Remove the hare and keep warm.

Add the shallots to the roasting pan and sauté (adding a little butter if necessary) until they are golden. Add the vinegar and boil to reduce by half. Add the cream and boil to reduce by about half. Season with salt and pepper.

Boil the fettuccine until it is cooked through, about 5 minutes. Drain and toss with the 3 tablespoons butter and a little thyme. Carve the hare and serve with the sauce and pasta.

Wine: Gevrey-Chambertin, Volnay, Pomerol, or a well-aged Bandol

SADDLE OF HARE WITH PEAR SAUCE AND SPICES

◆ ◆ ◆

Râble de lièvre sauce poire et épices

The saddle of hare is the part between the thighs and the neck. Usually most of the rib cage is trimmed away, leaving the two loins connected by the backbone. The French cook this cut of hare very rare. You may wish to cook it a little longer than the 14 minutes suggested.

Serves 4

2 trimmed saddles of hare
Salt and pepper
1 hare liver
1 onion
1 garlic clove
1 pear
3 tablespoons butter, plus
    more for sautéing
    (optional)
2 cloves

1-inch piece of cinnamon
    stick
2 pieces of dried orange rind
1½ teaspoons aged red wine
    vinegar
1½ teaspoons Port
1 cup heavy cream
1 teaspoon mustard
¼ teaspoon cocoa powder

Preheat the oven to 425° F.

Season the 2 saddles of hare with salt and pepper, set in a roasting pan, and roast for 12 to 14 minutes. Keep warm.

Chop the liver very fine with a knife. Slice the onion and garlic fine. Peel, core, and coarsely dice the pear.

Set the roasting pan over a moderate flame, add the onion and garlic, and sauté until softened (add a little butter if necessary). Add the cloves, cinnamon, and orange rind. Pour in the vinegar and cook until it has completely evaporated. Add the Port and cook to reduce by half. Add the cream and pear and boil to reduce by a third. Strain. Add the liver, mustard, and cocoa to the sauce and heat briefly, without letting it boil. Gradually add the 3 tablespoons butter, stirring continually. Strain once again. Keep warm.

Cut the loins of the hare from the skeleton and then slice across the grain. Season with coarsely ground pepper and serve with the sauce spooned around.

You can accompany the hare with a raw spinach salad or a puree of either chestnuts, celery root (celeriac), or sweet potatoes.

Wine: Serve the same wines as you would for the roast hare (see preceding recipe) or an Hermitage or Côte-Rôtie

FOLLOWING
THE GAME

◆ ◆ ◆

Robert Ardrey, in his stimulating book
Et la chasse créa l'homme, *explains*
that "hunting created man"
by showing that if vegetarian primates
had never learned to kill, they could not have become human.
It was under Clotaire III, in 656,
that the patron saint of hunters was born.

◆◆◆

Hubert, while hunting on Good Friday in 683, saw a crucifix appear in the antlers of a stag as if to reproach him for killing on the day that commemorated Christ's death. In the tenth century, this great-grandson of Clovis would become the patron saint of hunters.

The meat from game is very interesting because it contains very little fat—about 2 percent, compared to 22 percent in beef, 25 percent in lamb shoulder, and 10 percent in loin of veal, with about the same amount of protein. I speak here of "real" game, which is, alas, seldom found. Unfortunately, more and more chefs have sold out to raised game, to farmed animals with more fat and surely less flavor.

The combination of game and wine should encourage you to uncork a fine bottle. Its rich aroma will go marvelously with the taste of the meat. But above all you will discover a rare accord of structure and body in your mouth. With wild boar, venison, hare, wild duck, or woodcock, choose among Vougeot, Richebourg, Grands-Echezeaux, Aloxe-Corton, and Pommard. You will be equally happy with a wine from the Côtes-du-Rhône such as Châteauneuf-du-Pape, Côte-Rôtie, or Hermitage.

Bordeaux such as Pomerols or Pauillacs will seduce you with harmonies of the utmost finesse. I would also recommend the (less costly) great Spanish wines of Rioja.

For feathered game, choose a more delicate wine, such as Chambolle-Musigny, Beaune, Volnay, or from Bordeaux—in addition to the ones mentioned above—Margaux.

There are numerous species of wild duck, among which the best known and appreciated in France is the *colvert*. You can find it from mid-July until February, but it is best at the beginning of the season, when it is young. You can recognize this species by its flexible beak. Before eating, you should leave it in cold storage, unplucked, hung by its head, for 2 to 4 days.

ROAST WILD DUCK

◆ ◆ ◆

Canard sauvage rôti

Cooking time will vary depending on the size of the wild duck you use. In France, duck is eaten very rare, so that cooking time would be about 5 minutes per pound. If you wish your duck breast to be pink rather than rare, increase cooking time to about 7 minutes per pound. Mousse de foie gras *is available in specialty stores.*

Serves 4

2 young wild ducks	1 tablespoon *mousse de foie*
1 medium-sized carrot	*gras*
1 medium-sized onion	Dijon mustard
1 unpeeled garlic clove	2 teaspoons chopped fresh
Salt and pepper	coriander
Oil	Bread crumbs
Butter	Green or white peppercorns
2 cups dry red wine	Coarse sea salt

Preheat the oven to 475° F.

Cut the wings off the ducks at the first joint closest to the body. Using a heavy chef's knife or cleaver, chop the wings and necks into several pieces. Reserve the livers. Tie together the legs of each duck. Peel the carrot and onion and chop into large pieces. Spread these along with the chopped wings, necks, and garlic in the bottom of a roasting pan. Set the ducks on top and sprinkle with salt, pepper, and about 2 teaspoons oil mixed with 2 teaspoons melted butter. Place in the oven and roast for 15 to 20 minutes. Baste occasionally with a little more of the oil and butter mixture. When the ducks are cooked, the juices will still be very pink. Remove the ducks from the pan and keep warm. Deglaze the pan by pouring in the red wine. Set over high heat and boil until the liquid has reduced by three quarters. Strain.

Purée the duck livers in a blender; stir in the *mousse de foie gras* and ½ teaspoon mustard. Stir this mixture into the wine reduction. Heat this sauce over low heat, stirring continually. Do not allow it to boil. Adjust the seasoning and add the coriander.

Preheat the oven to 400° F.

Cut the legs off the ducks, brush each with mustard, and then dip in the bread crumbs. Set on a roasting pan, sprinkle lightly with butter, and bake in the preheated oven for 10 to 15 minutes. Carve the breasts and serve with the sauce. Sprinkle with coarsely ground green or white peppercorns and coarse sea salt. Serve with a garnish of sliced apples sauteed in butter or with noodles.

Serve the warm duck legs as a second course accompanied by a salad.

WILD DUCK WITH SPINACH

◆ ◆ ◆

Aiguillettes et cuisses
de canard sauvage aux épinards

If you cannot find ducks as small as 1½ pounds, simply substitute a larger 3–4-pound wild duck and roast for approximately 20 minutes longer.

Serves 4

2 wild ducks (each about 1½ pounds)
Salt and pepper
Butter
1 pound spinach
2 navel oranges
1 tablespoon sherry vinegar
½ tablespoon aged red wine vinegar

4 tablespoons peanut oil
2 tablespoons chopped herbs (equal parts of parsley, chervil, and chives)
2 tablespoons chopped shallot

Preheat the oven to 425° F.

Season the ducks with salt and pepper. Roast, breast side up, for 13 minutes, then turn them over and continue cooking for an additional 25 minutes. Baste with a little butter and any accumulated juices.

Wash the spinach, remove the stems, and dry well. Slice in ½-inch strips. Peel the oranges and separate into sections. Stir together the 2 vinegars, the oil, and salt and pepper to taste.

Heat the serving platter. Take the ducks out of the oven, remove their legs, and cut them in half at the joint. Remove the breast meat and slice. Sprinkle lightly with salt and pepper.

Toss the spinach with the herbs, shallot, oranges, and vinaigrette. Spread the salad on the serving platter and arrange the duck parts on top.

THE MYSTERY
OF THE TRUFFLE

◆ ◆ ◆

"Plant engendered by the autumn rains,
accompanied by peals of thunder."
It was thus that Theophrastus,
writing in the third century B.C.,
described this strange fruit of the earth
that we call the truffle.

Everyone is mistaken: it isn't a mushroom that is gathered but rather its "fruit." The genuine mushroom consists of a plant body, or thallus, which comes up from a system of filaments called the mycelium.

The truffle, a fungus of the genus *Tuber*, fascinated the ancients, who believed that this black diamond was spontaneously generated and named it "child of the gods." Some defended this belief until the beginning of the twentieth century. Others have claimed that the truffle came from the branches of a tree. There have been those who long maintained the hypothesis that truffles were simply a gall brought on by a fly bite on a tree's roots. In any case, when it comes to truffles, it pays to be wary, since there exist some seventy varieties around the world, of which thirty-two grow in Europe. Some, such as the "truffle of the desert" (the Libyan truffle), which is surely the variety cited by the ancients, has little in common with the true *Tuber melanosporum*, known as the Périgord truffle. The name refers to a botanical variety which may or may not come from the region of Périgord.

Périgord truffles have been closely connected with vine cultivation. Toward the middle of the nineteenth century, the Périgord plateau, the Sarladais, and other regions, all the way to Argentat (Corrèze), consisted of vineyards covering some 275,000 acres. At that time, truffles were little more than an "accessory" resource. The growers, in order to protect their plants, had to dig ditches alongside the vines that grew near oak trees in order to isolate them from encroachment by truffles.

However, in 1868–72, the Phylloxera epidemic destroyed the region's vineyards, leaving only the truffles in place. The harvest statistics of the time are a wonder: 400, 600, even 1,100 pounds of truffles from just one property! In 1912, the regions of Périgord and Quercy marketed 280 tons, and total French production attained 800 tons. In 1986, the entire nation's harvest was a mere 30 tons.

On New Year's Eve of 1664, Molière was supping at the house of Mme de Sévigné in the company of Cardinal Legat, a jovial and spirited Italian gourmet. On seeing a splendid platter of truffles, the latter couldn't hold back a contented exclamation in his maternal tongue: *"Tartuffoli!"* The word so pleased Molière, who had been searching for an original name for the principal character of his new play, that he decided to call him Tartuffe.

TRUFFLES WITH SALT

◆ ◆ ◆

Truffes à la croque-au-sel

Only truffles gathered between December and March—after the first frost and before spring returns—should be served in this way. Brush the fresh truffles to remove the dirt, then peel and cut into thick slices. Serve with fresh sweet or lightly salted butter. You could also serve bread lightly brushed with goose fat and garlic, then toasted. Place the truffle slices on the bread and serve with a green salad dressed with olive oil and lemon.

Wines: A Pauillac (such as Château Lynch-Bages, 1975) or a Coteaux-des-Baux-de-Provence (for example, Domaine de Trévalon, 1983)

TRUFFLE ROLLS

◆ ◆ ◆

Pain aux truffes

You will have enough dough to make a dozen rolls from this recipe. It is much easier to make the larger quantity. Chef Senderens recommends that you make the leftover dough into one large loaf, which you can eat later: for example, toasted for breakfast the following day.

Makes 4 small truffle rolls

2 cups white wheat bread flour	1 cup lukewarm water
¾ cup rye flour	¾ teaspoon salt
1¼ teaspoons active dry yeast	4 truffles, each about 10 grams (about ¼ ounce)

Sift together the flours. Dissolve the yeast in ½ cup of the water and the salt in the other half. Combine all of this in a bowl and stir until completely combined. Scoop the dough onto a floured board and knead until smooth, about 10 minutes. Divide the dough into 3 equal pieces and then divide 1 of those pieces into 4 equal balls. Enfold a truffle in the center of each of these 4. Place these rolls on a baking sheet and, using a vaporizer, spray every 10 minutes with water. Let rise about 45 minutes in a warm place, or until they have doubled in volume.

Preheat the oven to 500° F.

Dust the tops of the rolls with flour and lightly slash the top of each with a razor blade.

Set the baking sheet in the center of the oven and bake about 15 to 20 minutes. It is best to allow the bread to rest for 30 minutes and then to reheat it briefly before serving. This will allow the truffles to perfume the bread.

Wine: Red Côtes-du-Rhône (such as Château de Fonsalette), red Châteauneuf-du-Pape

TRUFFLE AND

FOIE GRAS TURNOVERS

◆ ◆ ◆

Chaussons aux truffes et foie gras

Serves 4

6 ounces puff pastry*
4 truffles, each about 10
    grams (¼ ounce)
1 egg, lightly beaten

1 head *frisée* or curly endive
4 slices foie gras terrine or
    canned foie gras

Roll out the puff pastry on a floured board to about ⅛ inch thickness. Cut out 4 (6-inch) circles, set a truffle in the center of each, brush the edges of the pastry with the egg, and fold the dough in half to form a half-moon shape. Pinch the edges of the dough to make sure the truffles are fully enclosed. Decorate the turnovers by making a lattice pattern with thin strips of the remaining dough. Brush with the egg.

Preheat the oven to 400° F.

Bake the turnovers on a baking sheet for about 15 minutes, until puffed and golden. Serve accompanied by a salad of the *frisée*, lightly dressed with a vinaigrette (see Appendix) and

* This is available in specialty stores and some supermarkets.

topped with the foie gras slices. You can also sprinkle a few truffle shavings over the salad.

Wine: A Pauillac or a red Châteauneuf-du-Pape

TRUFFLE CONSERVES

◆ ◆ ◆

Conserves de truffes

Makes 1 pint

¾ pound truffles   2 tablespoons Port

Clean and dry the truffles. Fill a pint mason jar with them, then add the Port. Screw the top loosely on the jar. Submerge the jar completely in boiling water and simmer for 1 hour 40 minutes. Remove from the water, screw the top tight, and allow to cool completely. This will keep for months. Use as a garnish or as a substitute for fresh truffles.

FABULOUS FUNGUS

◆ ◆ ◆

Who, in France, does not know the cèpe,
this king of mushrooms?
In fact, there are some sixty-five
varieties of differing quality,
though almost all are edible.
For the following recipes choose the
most flavorful, with flesh that is thick, white, and firm,
possessing a fruity aroma.

◆◆◆

The French enthusiast calls them *cèpes*, and the mycologist, *Boletus*. Because they are so easily identified, dangerous mistakes seldom occur, and commercially sold mushrooms are always checked by experts. However, they are frequently prey to worms and moldiness. They should always be very fresh, neither emaciated nor obese. The genuine *cèpe* is the *Boletus edulis* or *cèpe de Bordeaux*. There is also the dark brown *cèpe* (*tête-de-nègre*) known as *Boletus aereus*.

Cèpes are affected by and grow in the vicinity of particular types of trees and forests: beeches and oaks, chestnuts, pines and other conifers—each have their own kind of *cèpe*, as do plain and mountain. The texture may be more or less dense, with a specific taste that varies from nutty to musky to sweet. Do not wash the mushrooms and do not peel them; simply wipe them with a damp cloth. The bottom of each stem should be pared, since it is often full of earth.

Reserve the stems for stuffings or hashes. They can be dried and then may be ground to a powder, kept separately or mixed with other mushrooms and spices. Store them in an airtight jar. They will serve you well for flavoring savory pastries or sauces.

Sort the *cèpes*, setting aside the largest, oldest, and softest ones. You can stuff these or use them for enhancing a sauce or stuffing. The firm small ones should be prepared without delay.

STUFFED *CÈPES*

◆ ◆ ◆

Cèpes farcis

or Portobello

This recipe can be made with any large mushroom. Portobello mushrooms work particularly well. If you use these, you will probably find that you need to add more liquid during cooking.

Fresh and dried Boletus edulis are available in North America under the name of Boletes, or more often under their Italian designation porcini. *They are also occasionally called* cèpes.

Serves 4

4 fresh *cèpes*, each about 6 ounces	4 tablespoons chopped parsley
¾ cup milk	2 cloves garlic, chopped
1½ cups bread crumbs	2 teaspoons oil
6 ounces prosciutto	2 tablespoons chicken broth (optional)
6 ounces meat cut from cured pigs' trotters or boiled ham	Juice of 1 lemon or aged red wine vinegar
2 eggs	

Remove the mushroom stems. Stir together the milk and bread crumbs. Chop the prosciutto and ham and mix with the bread-milk mixture and the eggs, parsley, and garlic. Fill the mushroom caps with this mixture. Heat the oil in a shallow flameproof casserole over moderate heat. Add the mushrooms and brown lightly on the bottom. Add about 2 tablespoons water or, better yet, chicken broth, cover, and cook over very low heat for about 1 hour. Check every 15 minutes and add more liquid if necessary. Before serving, sprinkle with lemon juice or aged red wine vinegar.

GRILLED *CÈPES*

◆ ◆ ◆

Cèpes grillés

Serves 4

4 *cèpes*, each about 6 ounces	Lemon juice
Oil	Salt
¼ cup softened butter	Foie gras (optional)
2 tablespoons chopped parsley	

Remove the mushroom stems. Slice each cap into 2 or 3 rounds. Brush with a little oil and grill or broil over a moderate flame.

Make a *maître d'hôtel* butter by stirring together the butter, parsley, and a few drops of lemon juice. Season the mushrooms only with salt, since *cèpes* do not take well to pepper.

Top with the butter or, better yet, with warm or cold foie gras. Serve with a little salad.

CÈPES MARINATED IN OLIVE OIL

◆ ◆ ◆

Cèpes marinés à l'huile d'olive

Serves 3 to 4

2 pounds *cèpes*	1 tablespoon white
2 cups dry white wine	peppercorns
1 teaspoon salt	3 cloves
2 bay leaves, coarsely	4 cups olive oil
crushed	

Choose firm, intact *cèpes* without any blemishes. Cut into ¾-inch cubes. Combine the 2 cups white wine with the salt and ½ cup water in a non-reactive, flameproof casserole. Bring to a boil, add the *cèpes*, return to a boil, and continue cooking 3 or 4 minutes. Drain and dry on a linen cloth.

Sterilize 3 (1-pint) mason jars by plunging them into boiling water for 30 seconds. Dry thoroughly. When the mushrooms are fully dry, start layering them in the glass jars. Add a little bay leaf and pepper to each layer. Place 1 clove in each jar. When the jars are full, pour in the olive oil, making sure there are no air pockets. Seal. In 2 or 3 days, add a little more oil if necessary. Check periodically to make sure the mushrooms are always fully covered with oil.

The mushrooms will keep for months. Serve as an appetizer, in salads, or as is.

CÈPE STEW

◆ ◆ ◆

Civet de cèpes

Serves 6

4½ pounds large *cèpes*
Oil
1 large slice of baked ham,
   about 6 ounces
3 shallots

Lard
4 cups red wine
Salt and pepper
Fine bread crumbs

Clean the mushrooms. Remove the caps and wipe clean. Peel the stems and chop coarsely. Heat 1 tablespoon oil in a large skillet, add the mushroom caps, and cook until lightly browned. Dice the ham and chop the shallots. In a large flame-proof casserole, combine about 1 tablespoon lard (or peanut oil), the ham, shallots, and mushroom stems. Sauté briefly. Add the wine and bring to a boil. Add the caps to this mixture; add a little salt and just a touch of pepper. Simmer for 1 hour. Just before serving, stir in about ¼ cup bread crumbs, or just enough to thicken the sauce.

This *civet* goes well with roast veal, game, and kidneys though you can certainly serve it on its own, accompanied by a good Pomerol.

CÈPE CREAM SAUCE

◆ ◆ ◆

Crème de cèpes

You could substitute about 3 ounces dried cèpes for the fresh in this recipe. Cover the dried mushrooms with 1 cup cool water and let soak ½ hour. Drain, reserving the liquid, and carefully rinse off any sand. Pass the soaking liquid through a coffee filter to remove any dirt. Sauté the mushrooms, add the soaking liquid, and boil until almost no liquid remains; then continue as below. Chef Senderens suggests serving the sauce with chicken, crayfish, or scallops.

Serves 6

1 pound fresh *cèpes*	Salt and white pepper
3 tablespoons butter	1 teaspoon lemon juice
3 cups heavy cream	

Wipe the *cèpes* and remove any dirt. Cut into fine slices. Melt the butter in a non-reactive, flameproof saucepan over moderate heat, add the mushrooms, and cook until they cease to give off liquid. Add the cream and simmer until the sauce thickens. It should reduce by about half. Strain through a fine sieve, pressing down on the mushrooms to extract as much liquid as possible. Discard the drained *cèpes*. Season with salt and pepper and the lemon juice.

TUBER

OF THE

RISING SUN

◆ ◆ ◆

Born of the Far East,
the so-called Japanese artichokes
embarked for Europe at the end of the last century.
In Paris, they would be famous.
Their hour of glory had come.

This tuber (*Stachys tuberifera*), which belongs to the family of the Labiatae—its delicate flavor reminiscent of artichoke and salsify—came to us from China. It had been grown there since time immemorial under the names *tignou-tze* and *kan-lou*. In an article by Flanchet, who had made a study of the cultivation of Japanese flora, the magazine *Le Jardin*, in 1889, informs us that it had apparently never been seen in a wild state in Japan. However, it was cultivated there, though rarely, under the exotic names *tsyo rogi* and *chorogi*.

The introduction to France of the Japanese artichoke (also known as Chinese artichoke or *crosne du Japon*) dates to 1882, but it did not meet with much success until five years later. (It paralleled an event of an entirely different dimension: Parisians saw, that year, the sprouting of the Eiffel Tower, which noted spokesmen of the time described, with a malicious wink, as the greatest piece of hardware ever built.) It was a certain Dr. Breitschneider, physician to the Russian legation in Peking, who sent the tuber to the Société d'Acclimatation, care of Fathers Bois and Pailleux. And it was the latter who planted the specimens near his residence in Crosne, a village in the

Essonne. In the winter of 1886/87, he harvested 6,750 pounds of them. Convinced that trying to commercialize the product under its real name, *Stachys*, was doomed to failure, he preferred to baptize it *crosne*. And in order to make it sound exotic, he followed it with the qualifier *du Japon* ("of Japan"). Thanks to a vigorous campaign, orders poured in from all the large cities in the country and even from abroad. The tubers were destined for high society, so that its members could boast that they had tasted this oddly shaped root with its fine and delicate flavor. Chinese poets had sung their praise in the fifteenth century as "rings of jade bound together and yet mobile."

However, very soon, the plant's fecundity made it lose much of its prestige among those who sought it out precisely for its rarity. Chinese artichokes rapidly found their way from luxurious food boutiques to greengrocers' carts and markets, among all the other vegetables accessible to every pocketbook. In the department of Meurthe-et-Moselle, they spread to the point of overwhelming the indigenous plants and incurred the wrath of the farmers. Oh, if only the same would come to pass with our beautiful and beloved truffle!

The fashion for this little vegetable is also due to Alexandre Dumas fils, who was as much a gastronome as a writer. He gave, in his play *Francillon*, a recipe for a "Japanese salad," though it was the restaurateur Brébant, well known at the time, who added Japanese artichokes to potatoes to make the salad more "Japanese." Dumas fils, in his *Grande Dictionnaire de cuisine*, does not speak of the Japanese artichoke, and for a good reason: the work was published in 1873. You can find the formula for the *Francillon* salad in Escoffier, that former chefs' bible: "Two parts potatoes, marinated in Chablis; one part mussels poached with celery, trimmed; and one part truffles. Season the potatoes sufficiently . . . to complement the dish."

SEAFOOD WITH

JAPANESE ARTICHOKES

◆ ◆ ◆

Cassolettes de fruits de mer
aux crosnes du Japon

Crosnes, or Japanese or Chinese artichokes, as they are called in English, are not commercially available in the United States. You could substitute Jerusalem artichokes for an analogous taste.

Serves 4

4 shallots	16 medium-sized clams
14 tablespoons butter	8 oysters
¼ cup Champagne	16 small clams
2 cups fish broth or clam juice	¾ pound Japanese artichokes
	1 tablespoon coarse salt
¾ cup heavy cream	½ pound sea scallops
Salt and white pepper	

Prepare the sauce. Chop the shallots. Sauté the shallots with 1 tablespoon butter in a non-reactive saucepan until translucent, but without letting them color. Add the Champagne and boil to evaporate completely. Add 1 cup of the broth or clam juice and boil to evaporate almost completely. Finally, add the cream and boil to reduce by two thirds. Set over low heat and gradually whisk in 12 tablespoons of the butter, piece by piece, until incorporated. Taste for salt and pepper; strain.

Open the clams and oysters, reserve the juices, discard the shells, and keep refrigerated.

Cut off the end of each Japanese artichoke with a small knife, then rub them with the coarse salt in a kitchen cloth. Rinse under cold running water for 5 minutes. Cook for 4 minutes in boiling water. Chill under cold running water, drain, and set aside. (If you are using Jerusalem artichokes, scrub them clean, cut into 1-inch dice, and boil until just tender, about 10 minutes.)

Heat the remaining tablespoon butter in a flameproof casserole, add the scallops, and cook briefly without browning. Add the remaining 1 cup broth or clam juice and cook over low heat for 4 minutes.

Add the remaining shellfish and the Japanese artichokes, as well as the sauce. If the dish isn't too salty, you can also add the liquid from the opened shellfish. Season with pepper. Do not let this mixture boil.

Serve hot in shallow bowls accompanied by a Riesling.

THE
APPOINTED HOUR

◆ ◆ ◆

Asparagus?
Delightful since time immemorial.
With butter or with vinaigrette?
The choice is yours.
But just for variety's sake,
do try my recipe for
asparagus à la meunière.

Historical evidence indicates that asparagus has been held in high regard in numerous countries throughout the centuries, excepting the Middle Ages. For Pliny, it was a marvel of gourmandise. Suetonius reports that Augustus was fond of the Latin locution "in less time than it takes to cook asparagus." Some two hundred years before Christ, Cato was already teaching trench cultivation, in which you begin the cultivation on top of a long mound. It continued to be practiced until the middle of the nineteenth century. During the Middle Ages, certain luxury vegetables which, in Europe, had only ever been of interest to the Romans, disappeared or were preserved solely in a few monasteries. Only the Syrians and Egyptians continued to grow asparagus, as did the Arabs in Spain, who were to reintroduce it there in the fourteenth and fifteenth centuries. It became fashionable once more during the Renaissance. It is said that Louis XIV "persecuted" his gardeners so that he would be able to eat asparagus as early as the month of December. And who doesn't know the story of Bernard Le Bovier de Fontenelle (1657–1757), philosopher and permanent secretary to the Academy of Sciences, who loved asparagus served with butter as much as his friend the Abbé Terranson was devoted to asparagus with vinaigrette? Having invited the latter for dinner, Fontenelle had arranged for half the asparagus to be served with butter and the other half with vinaigrette. On his way to the table, the abbé died suddenly, struck down by apoplexy, and Fontenelle is reported to have cried out to his cook, "Make it all with butter! Make it all with butter!"

Asparagus *à la Fontenelle* is served with melted butter and a soft-boiled egg, in which you successively dip each spear.

In France, there are three varieties of asparagus, their season extending from the beginning of March through the end of June. White asparagus, gathered as soon as it emerges from the ground, is grown in Alsace and Belgium; it is also imported from North Africa. It is large and soft and doesn't have much flavor. Purple asparagus, which is allowed to grow several inches above the ground, comes from Aquitaine, Charentes, and the Loire Valley, as well as Italy; it is delicious and fruity. Green asparagus is picked in the Rhône Valley when it measures some 6 inches; it is a luxurious vegetable, the most flavorful of all. There also exists wild asparagus: thin and green, slightly bitter, but very good.

Fresh asparagus should be rigid and crisp, with no brown spots, and with vibrantly colored tips. Wrapped in a damp cloth, it will last three days at the most. It is always eaten cooked, whether boiled or steamed; however, it may be served hot, warm, or cold. It is a vegetable low in calories—about 110 calories per pound—but rich in vitamins A and C. Good manners permit you to eat the tips with a fork and the rest with your fingers, or you may even eat the whole vegetable out of hand, in which case you should make finger bowls available.

ASPARAGUS WITH MUSHROOMS

◆ ◆ ◆

Asperges aux champignons de Paris meunière

Serves 4

½ pound small mushrooms
2 pounds asparagus
3 shallots
1 tablespoon white wine
  vinegar
Salt
3 tablespoons butter
Freshly ground pepper

1 tablespoon lemon juice
1 tablespoon chopped fresh
  chives
1 tablespoon chopped
  parsley
1 tablespoon chopped
  chervil

Cut off the bases of the mushrooms, leaving about ½ inch of stem; quarter each mushroom. Wash in cold running water, then dry in a kitchen towel. Cut off the woody part of the asparagus and, using a vegetable peeler, peel the bottom two thirds of each stalk, leaving the top intact. Wash and drain. Chop the shallots fine.

Bring about 1 gallon water to a boil. Add the vinegar and about 1 tablespoon salt. Bring to a rolling boil. If the asparagus stems vary a great deal in thickness, divide them into 3 bundles, each containing stalks of the same diameter. Tie each bundle with kitchen twine. Boil the asparagus for about 4 minutes if it is thin and up to 10 minutes if thick. Drain.

Heat 1 tablespoon of the butter in a large skillet. Add the asparagus and sauté for about 3 minutes, until lightly browned. Season with a little salt and pepper. (Always add the pepper at the last moment.) Transfer to a serving platter and keep warm.

Melt the remaining 2 tablespoons butter and sauté the mushrooms and shallots. Season with salt and pepper and spoon over the asparagus. Sprinkle with the lemon juice and chopped herbs. You can substitute morels or chanterelles for the domestic mushrooms.

Wine: Château-Chalon, Château-Grillet

STRAIGHT FROM THE HEART

◆ ◆ ◆

*The artichoke, close cousin
to the thistle and the cardoon,
was not really common in France until about 1916,
when its cultivation took hold, especially in Brittany.
From the smallest baby artichoke
to the largest globe artichoke,
it is a delicious summer vegetable.*

◆◆◆

I t was the Italians who spread artichokes throughout France. In 1473, they were considered a novelty in Venice. By 1557, they were already widely distributed throughout Tuscany, where, it is said, they had been introduced from Sicily. In France, artichokes were well known in the first half of the sixteenth century. Catherine de Médicis ate so many of them at one meal that she thought she would burst. Some have seen them as contributing to loose morals, since under the medieval theory of the four humors they are attributed with "heating" faculties.

Here is how *Le Chansonnier français* (1740) presented the vegetable: "Colin, while eating artichokes, says to his wife, 'Darling, have some, they are very fresh. On my honor, they are of the best variety.' The beauty, with gentle demeanor, says to him, 'You eat them, love of my heart, since I will thus gain greater benefit from them than if I were to eat them myself.'"

Artichokes are eaten from May to July. They should be of moderate size, with firm green leaves and, above all, with no brown spots. For whole cooked artichokes, don't cut the stem but rather break it off and pull down so that the fibers come out with the part you discard.

ARTICHOKE BOTTOMS
WITH COCKLES AND VEGETABLES

◆ ◆ ◆

Fonds d'artichaut aux coques
et brunoise aux légumes

Cockles, coques in French, are a kind of tiny, very sweet clam. They are occasionally carried by better fishmongers and can also often be found in larger Chinatowns. You could certainly substitute littleneck or steamer clams in this recipe.

Serves 4

2 large artichokes	Sprigs of parsley
⅓ cup flour	Bay leaf
Lemon juice	1 cup white wine
½ pound carrots	2 tablespoons butter
½ pound zucchini	2 cups *crème fraîche*
4 pounds cockles	Salt and pepper
2 onions	Chopped fresh chives
Thyme	

Remove most of the artichokes' outside leaves; trim the stems. Combine the flour and about 2 tablespoons lemon juice with 6 cups water in a large saucepan. Bring to a boil, add the artichoke hearts, and cook 20 minutes, until the artichoke bottoms can be easily pierced with a knife. Drain and cool. Remove any remaining leaves and scoop out the fuzzy chokes, leaving only the artichoke bottoms. Slice these fine.

Cut the carrots and zucchini in ¼-inch dice. Cook the vegetables separately in boiling water, about 6 minutes for the carrots and 3 for the zucchini. Drain and cool under cold running water. Blot dry on paper towels.

Soak the cockles in a large basin of salt water for an hour or 2, then wash in plenty of cold water. Slice 1 of the onions and combine with several sprigs of thyme and parsley, the bay leaf, and the wine in a large pot. Add the cockles, cover tightly, and set over moderately high heat. Steam until the shellfish have opened. Remove the cockles from their shells and keep warm. Strain the cooking liquid and reserve.

Chop the remaining onion fine. Melt the butter in a skillet over moderate heat. Add the chopped onion and sauté until soft and translucent. Add the carrots and zucchini and enough cockle cooking liquid to just cover the vegetables. Bring to a rapid boil and boil to reduce the liquid by half. Add the *crème fraîche*, and heat. Strain, reserving the vegetables. Return the cream mixture to the pan. Add ½ teaspoon fresh thyme leaves to this sauce, bring to a boil, and reduce by about half, until the sauce is thick enough to coat the back of a spoon. Season with salt and pepper.

To serve, spread the vegetable mixture in the center of a serving platter. Arrange the artichokes around this, place the cockles on top, and cover with the sauce. Decorate with a sprinkling of chopped chives.

Wine: Muscadet, Alsatian Riesling, Chablis

MY RECIPE FOR

STUFFED ARTICHOKES

◆ ◆ ◆

Artichauts farcis à notre façon

Serves 6

6 globe artichokes	¾ pound sausage meat
5 lemons	2 egg yolks
⅔ cup flour	1 cup bread crumbs
¼ pound lean bacon	2 tablespoons chopped
2 onions	parsley
1 garlic clove	Salt and pepper
¼ pound duck foie gras	Butter

SAUCE

2 tablespoons *crème fraîche*	Chopped fresh chives
12 tablespoons butter	Salt and white pepper
Lemon juice	

Cut off the top half of each artichoke. Remove all the tough outside leaves and scoop out the center choke. Rub each artichoke with the juice of ½ lemon. In a large non-reactive saucepan, combine 10 cups water with the juice of the remaining 2 lemons and the flour. Bring to a boil, add the artichokes, and boil about 25 minutes. Remove the artichokes, set upside down, and drain well.

In the meantime, dice the bacon, chop the onion and garlic fine, and dice the foie gras. Fry the bacon in a skillet over moderate heat. Add the onion and garlic and cook until softened. Add the sausage meat and cook about 15 minutes, until it is cooked through. Add the egg yolks, ½ cup of the bread crumbs, the foie gras, and the parsley. Season with salt and pepper. Stuff the artichokes with this filling, sprinkle with the remaining ½ cup bread crumbs, and top each artichoke with a little butter.

Preheat the oven to 375° F.

Bake the artichokes for 15 to 20 minutes. Midway through cooking, add a little water to the pan so that they do not stick.

Prepare the sauce: heat the *crème fraîche* in a small saucepan over low heat. Gradually add the butter, a small piece at a time, stirring continually. Season with a few drops of lemon juice and about ½ teaspoon chopped chives. Season with salt and pepper.

To serve, place an artichoke on each plate and surround with the sauce. Serve hot.

Wine: Tokay d'Alsace (also known as Pinot Gris)

◆◆◆◆◆◆◆◆◆◆◆◆◆◆◆◆◆◆◆◆◆◆◆◆◆◆◆◆◆◆◆◆◆◆◆◆

BETA VULGARIS
(REFINED)

◆ ◆ ◆

So misunderstood, the beet!
Especially by those who confuse
sugar beets and beets grown for fodder
with the red beet, the only one that is edible.
Its superb red color
does wonders on a table—
and not merely as an appetizer.

I t was during the Renaissance that *Beta romana*, having been consumed since antiquity, was to know its first real success. It was so named because Italian growers had improved the strain and popularized its use in Europe, most notably in Germany, where beets were eaten cooked over coals, in a salad seasoned with pepper or accompanied by horseradish. For a long time they were confined to vegetable gardens until finally in the eighteenth century they began to be cultivated in open fields, though as animal feed. It was only at the beginning of the First Empire that the sugar beet industry took hold.

The presence of sugar in beets was first noted by Olivier de Serres in 1575, but left little impression on the world at large. In 1747, the German chemist Andreas Marggraf extracted and crystallized it. In 1796, his disciple Achard (of French Huguenot origin) perfected a refining process that won over the Prussian king. The English, conscious of their insular position, offered in vain to pay a chemist to manufacture beet sugar. They wished to ensure their independence in case Napoleon attempted a blockade to ruin the English economy.

The emperor ordered 80,000 acres of sugar beets to be

planted and announced that companies producing more than ten tons of sugar would be exempt from taxes for four years. The first sugar refinery was built at this time in Passy. When Napoleon visited this factory on January 2, 1812, he was so overcome with joy that he removed the Croix d'Honneur that he wore on his chest and handed it to Delessert, founder of this "sugar machine," saying, "This is worth ten victorious battles."

Beet roots, rich in sugar, vitamins, calcium, and mineral salts, are eaten raw, grated, or more commonly cooked and chilled, as an hors d'oeuvre, or, while still hot, in soup or as a garnish for poultry.

The varieties with elongated roots are sweeter and more aromatic than those with round ones. In France, they appear on the market mostly in the fall and winter, more often than not already cooked. You can, nevertheless, buy them raw and cook them in the ashes, or in the oven at 350° F. (This could take from 30 minutes to 2 hours depending on the size of the beets.) Beet roots can also be boiled in salted water to which a little vinegar has been added, 30 to 40 minutes for small ones and 2 to 2½ hours for really large ones, or 20 to 30 minutes in a pressure cooker. Make sure you do not pierce them during cooking because they will lose their juices. To test for doneness, rub the skin near the stem to see if it can be easily loosened. Peel them while they are still warm.

LAMB SWEETBREADS WITH
BEET AND BEAN SALAD

◆ ◆ ◆

*Ris d'agneau sur salade de betteraves rouges
et de haricots verts*

Serves 4

2 medium-sized beets
½ pound lamb sweetbreads
White wine vinegar
Salt
1½ tablespoons butter
Pepper
Paprika
½ teaspoon sugar

1 tablespoon aged red wine
　vinegar
2½ tablespoons peanut oil
½ pound string beans,
　cooked
¼ pound *mâche*
½ small onion
Chopped fresh chives

Cook the beets, peel, and cool.

Soak the sweetbreads for 2 hours in ice water. Bring 3 cups water to a boil; add about a tablespoon white wine vinegar and a large pinch of salt. Add the sweetbreads, bring to a boil, and simmer 8 minutes. Drain and cool under cold running water. Clean the sweetbreads of any fat and slice. Heat the butter in a skillet over moderately high heat, add the sweetbreads, and brown. Season with salt, pepper, and a little paprika.

Cut the beets in thin slices; sprinkle with the sugar and a little white wine vinegar. Stir together the red wine vinegar and oil. Season with salt and pepper. Toss half of this vinaigrette with the beans. Clean, wash, and dry the *mâche* and toss with the remaining vinaigrette. Slice the onion fine.

To serve, place a mound of *mâche* in the center of each plate, top with the string beans and surround with alternating pieces of beet and sweetbreads. Sprinkle with the onion and chives. You can serve the beets and beans either warm or cold.

Wine: White Saint-Péray or white Saint-Joseph

TUNA WITH BEET SAUCE

◆ ◆ ◆

Thon à la betterave

To make the sauce, you will need to use an electric juicer. Alternately, your neighborhood health food store may sell beet juice.

Serves 4

3-inch piece of fresh ginger
2 lemons
8 shiitake mushrooms
⅓ cup beet juice
½ pound butter
Salt and pepper

1 tablespoon lemon juice
4 tuna steaks, each about ½ pound
1 tablespoon chopped fresh chives

Peel the ginger, cut it into thin slices across the grain, and then into thin julienne strips. Bring about 2 cups water to a boil, add the ginger, and simmer for 20 minutes. Drain. Using a vegetable peeler, remove the zest from the lemons, slice into julienne strips, and cook like the ginger—but only for 10 minutes. Remove the stems from the shiitake mushrooms and cut the caps in very thin strips. Simmer the beet juice in a small saucepan until it has reduced by half. Over very low heat, gradually stir in the butter, a small piece at a time. Season with salt, pepper, and the lemon juice. Remove from heat but keep slightly warm.

Broil or grill the tuna until medium-done; it should still be a little pink in the center. To serve, spoon some of the sauce on each plate. Set the tuna on top and garnish with the ginger, lemon zest, and raw mushrooms. Sprinkle with the chives.

You could substitute another fish for the tuna or even use chicken breasts.

Wine: Cassis, white Côtes-de-Provence

◆◆◆◆◆◆◆◆◆◆◆◆◆◆◆◆◆◆◆◆◆◆◆◆◆◆◆◆◆◆◆◆◆◆◆◆

SALAD DAYS

◆ ◆ ◆

A green salad or a composed salad?
Simple or complex, traditional or exotic,
it has to avoid chaos
and find the right balance
with its dressing: all an art.

◆◆◆◆◆◆◆◆◆◆◆◆◆◆◆◆◆◆◆◆◆◆◆◆◆◆◆◆◆◆◆◆◆◆◆◆◆◆

Salad, in the greater sense of the word, can certainly be a meal in itself (see the recipe for *Pot-au-feu* Salad, page 92). Here are five new recipes to suit every taste and to prove that a salad can be the most varied dish of all.

ENDIVE SALAD WITH SMOKED
SALMON AND HORSERADISH

◆ ◆ ◆

Salade d'endives au saumon et au raifort

Serves 4

4 large Belgian endives
1 large cucumber
½ pound smoked salmon
½ teaspoon Dijon mustard
1 tablespoon aged red wine
 vinegar

3 tablespoons olive oil
Salt and pepper
1 tablespoon chopped chives
⅓ cup *crème fraîche*
1 tablespoon grated fresh
 horseradish

Reserve 16 small leaves from the endive and slice the rest into strips. Peel the cucumber, remove the seeds, and slice thin. Cut the salmon in strips. Stir together the mustard, vinegar, and olive oil to make a vinaigrette. Season with salt and pepper. Toss a third of the vinaigrette with the cucumbers and the rest with the sliced endive and chives. Stir together the *crème fraîche* and horseradish.

To serve, mound sliced endive in the center of each plate, place the salmon on top, surround with the cucumber, and arrange 4 endive leaves, symmetrically, pointing out, around the outside. Spoon a little of the horseradish sauce between the endive leaves.

SPINACH SALAD WITH
SMOKED SALMON

◆ ◆ ◆

Salade de pousses d'épinards au saumon

Serves 4

1 pound spinach	4 thin slices of smoked
6 ounces mushrooms	salmon
Lemon juice	1 tablespoon chopped chives
⅔ cup *crème fraîche*	1 tablespoon chopped dill
1 teaspoon Dijon mustard	1 tablespoon toasted sesame
Salt and white pepper	seeds

Clean the spinach by removing the stems and washing in abundant cold water. Dry well. Slice the mushrooms and sprinkle with lemon juice so they do not discolor. Stir together the *crème fraîche*, mustard, and a tablespoon lemon juice, and season with salt and pepper. Cut the salmon into strips.

To serve, arrange the spinach leaves on a platter and top with the dressing. Sprinkle with the mushrooms, salmon, chives, dill, and finally the sesame seeds.

CURRIED CHICKEN SALAD

◆ ◆ ◆

Salade de poulet au curry

Serves 4

4 boneless chicken breasts
Salt and pepper
1 tablespoon butter
1 teaspoon fresh thyme
  leaves
1 teaspoon paprika
1 teaspoon curry powder
1 teaspoon *quatre-épices* (*see
  note, page 54*)
1 teaspoon five-spice powder
  (*see note, page 101*)

1 large pinch Cayenne
  pepper
6 ounces green beans
1 small celery root (celeriac)
1 pound mixed baby salad
  greens
1 avocado
4 large mushrooms

MAYONNAISE

1 egg yolk
⅓ cup olive oil
⅔ cup peanut oil

Salt and pepper
1 teaspoon curry powder

Preheat the oven to 375° F.

Sprinkle the breasts with salt and pepper. Heat the butter
in a flameproof casserole. Add the chicken and brown lightly.
Sprinkle with the thyme and spices and bake in the preheated
oven for 10 to 15 minutes. Chill.

Steam or boil the green beans, cool under cold running
water, and drain well.

Make a mayonnaise by beating the egg yolk with a wire
whisk and incorporating the oils very gradually, beating the
whole time. Season with salt, pepper, and the curry powder.

Peel the celery root, cut into thin julienne strips, and toss
with about a third of the mayonnaise.

Wash and dry the salad greens and place in the center of each plate. Slice the chicken breasts and arrange on top. Cut the avocado into quarters. Slice the mushrooms fine. Distribute the beans, avocado, and mushrooms around the chicken. Place little mounds of the celery root around the perimeter of the plate. Brush the meat and vegetables with a little of the curried mayonnaise.

SKATE SALAD WITH CAPERS

◆ ◆ ◆

Salade de raie aux câpres

Serves 4

1 small leek	1 lemon
1 small onion	1 tablespoon sherry vinegar
1 celery stalk	1 tablespoon aged red wine
2 sprigs of parsley	vinegar
2 sprigs of thyme	5 tablespoons peanut oil
½ cup dry white wine	5 tablespoons capers
Salt and pepper	1 head Boston lettuce
1 skate wing, about	1 tablespoon chopped chives
2 pounds	

Slice the leek and wash well. Slice the onion and celery. Combine these with the parsley, thyme, white wine, and 3 cups water in a large shallow saucepan. Season with salt and pepper. Bring to a boil and simmer 10 minutes. Add the skate wing and poach 15 to 20 minutes. Remove the skin (if the skate hasn't been skinned) and the central bone.

Using a vegetable peeler, remove the zest from the lemon; slice into julienne strips. Plunge into boiling water for 30 seconds, drain, and cool under cold running water.

Stir together the 2 vinegars, oil, and capers. Season with salt and pepper.

To serve, line each plate with lettuce leaves, arrange the warm fish on top, and sauce with the vinaigrette. Sprinkle with the lemon zest and chives.

GRILLED SUMMER VEGETABLE SALAD

◆ ◆ ◆

Salade d'été grillée

Serves 4

2 large red bell peppers	½ tablespoon dried oregano
2 garlic cloves	1 tablespoon walnut oil
Thyme	Pepper
2 bay leaves	1 large eggplant (about
Salt	1 pound)
Olive oil	1 pound zucchini
1 whole head garlic	4 small ripe tomatoes
1 egg yolk	½ small onion
1 tablespoon chopped fresh	1 small head Boston lettuce
thyme	
1 tablespoon chopped	
parsley	

Preheat the oven to 275° F.

Put the red peppers in a small roasting pan with the 2 garlic cloves, a little thyme, and the bay leaves. Sprinkle lightly with salt. Add ⅔ cup water and ⅓ cup olive oil. Set in the preheated oven and bake for 2 hours. Peel and remove the stem and seeds. Cut into strips.

Brush the garlic head with a little olive oil, wrap in aluminum foil, and bake in the 275° F. oven for 1 hour. Cut the garlic in half through the middle and squeeze each half to extract the cooked garlic cloves. Discard the peel. Stir together the garlic puree, the egg yolk, chopped thyme, parsley, and oregano. Stir in the walnut oil and gradually whisk in 5 tablespoons olive oil. Season with salt and pepper.

Slice the eggplant and zucchini lengthwise ¼ inch thick. Brush lightly with olive oil and broil or grill for about 4 minutes per side. Cut the tomatoes in quarters. Slice the onion fine.

To serve, line each plate with lettuce leaves and arrange the vegetables on top. Sprinkle with the onion and top with a ribbon of the garlic mayonnaise.

DRESSED
IN GREEN

◆ ◆ ◆

In salad, there is salt.
The word comes from the Latin herba salata,
meaning "salted herb," which gives an idea
of the first salads:
freshly picked vegetables
eaten with a little salt . . .
sophistication worthy of the gods.

◆◆

Why do we season our lettuce with a combination of oil, vinegar, and mustard? According to an English author (in *Monthly Repertory*, June 1810, page 362), this practice originated in Judah. In order to make the bitter herbs ritually eaten with the paschal lamb more palatable, the Hebrews (according to Morses Kotsensis) dressed them with a thick, viscous sauce called *karosett*, which consisted of a base of vinegar, mustard, and date oil or grapeseed oil. Maimonides added salt and pepper, which proves that he had unfailing taste and was worthy of making salad for the princes of his nation.

The ancient Greeks were familiar with the beneficial effects of salad, a dish which, according to them, was featured on the dining table of Olympus. In ancient Rome, salads were very elaborate. In the writings of Apicius, who lived in the first century B.C., we find dishes composed of raw vegetables and fresh or dried herbs, seasoned with vinegar, oil, and a salty fish extract known as *liquamen*, which may well recall the anchovies added to our own modern salads.

Elegant as ever, Brillat-Savarin said of salad in 1825: "It refreshes without making feeble, invigorates without irritating, and rejuvenates us."

A salad can be the most varied of dishes. The ingredients can be cooked or raw, or both. The very symbol of freshness, a salad finds itself regenerated with the coming of each season and plays with all its produce: green vegetables, or fish or meat, at times with fruit, to say nothing of salads made with a base of pasta, legumes, or cereals. Composed salads give free rein to the imagination, and here you can certainly show off your talents; it isn't merely that the possible mixtures are countless but that there is also the magic of seasoning, which intervenes, with different oils used separately or in combination. The same is true for vinegars. A pinch of a spice or herb and you are transported halfway around the planet while remaining at your table.

Too often, salad personifies the banality of the everyday at its most boring. This is precisely why this kind of dish can benefit from free improvisation, opening itself to poetry, without one's having to devote much effort, work, or time.

THE ART OF SEASONING SALAD

Restore its magic. It is a specialty so French that it allowed the Chevalier d'Albignac to buy himself a château in Limousin! This nobleman, who lived as an émigré in London during the Revolution, became a "salad maker," turning it into his profession. He used to go from house to house at the time salad was served, we are told by Brillat-Savarin: "Soon he had a carriage to transport him to the various districts where he had been called, and a servant used to carry a mahogany case that contained all the ingredients with which he had enriched his repertoire, such as scented vinegars, flavored and unflavored oils, caviar, truffles, anchovies, 'catchup' ["catchup" is the contemporary spelling of ketchup; this English condiment was already known in the nineteenth century], and concentrated meat juices."

"Venus lay down on a bed of lettuce in order to endure the loss of her Adonis and to calm herself." Is this why Galen called

it the "herb of the wise" and never lost an occasion to recommend taking a decoction brewed of the vegetable as an aid
to sleep?

And somewhat closer to our time, Victor Hugo, in *Les Mi-
sérables*, said: "Gavroche has his own point of view, his own
resentments, which are based in his hate of the bourgeois; his
own metaphors: to be dead means to eat dandelions from the
root up . . ."

GREEN BEAN SALAD

WITH PIMIENTOS

◆ ◆ ◆

Salade de haricots verts et poivrons confits

*If you cannot find the very thin green beans often sold in this country
under the French name* haricots verts, *regular string beans will work
perfectly well.*

Serves 4

2 red bell peppers	⅓ cup wine vinegar
2 bay leaves	⅔ cup peanut oil
2 garlic cloves	Salt and pepper
⅔ cup olive oil	2 tablespoons chopped herbs
1¼ pounds green beans	(a combination of fresh
2 shallots	tarragon, chives, and
1 teaspoon mustard	parsley)

Using the peppers, bay leaves, garlic, and ⅓ cup of the olive
oil, prepare them as in the recipe for Grilled Summer Vegetable
Salad (page 195).

Trim the beans. Bring 8 cups salted water to a rapid boil
and add the beans. Cook until tender but still a brilliant green,

about 5 minutes. Drain and cool under cold running water. Drain well.

Chop the shallots. Make the vinaigrette by stirring together the shallots, mustard, and vinegar. Gradually stir in the remaining ⅓ cup olive oil and the peanut oil. Season with salt and pepper and stir in the chopped herbs.

To serve, mound the beans in the center of a serving platter, arrange the pepper in the form of a star on top, and sauce with the vinaigrette. You may not need all of it.

A HOMELY
FLOWER

◆ ◆ ◆

In spite of its sincere appearance
and the docility with which
it submits to cooking,
the cauliflower remains unloved.
All the same, it serves as a fertile ground
for culinary art.

◆◆◆

The cauliflower appears to have degenerated from the large-headed cabbage and to have originated in the Levant. It used to go under the name Cyprus cabbage, and for a long time the seeds came from this island. It is mentioned, as Syrian cabbage, in the works of Arab botanists in Spain. The Genoese were known to grow the best cauliflowers, as a consequence of their maritime commerce with the Orient. While it had been prized in Greece and known in Rome, the vegetable later fell into disgrace, until Jean de La Quintinie reacclimatized it to Versailles. Louis XIV was passionately fond of it, cooked in bouillon flavored with nutmeg, and served with fresh butter: a recipe as current now as it was then, and worthy of Curnonsky, the chef and writer, who used to say: ". . . in which things taste of that which they are."

Eat your cauliflower. It has a mere 40 calories per 4-ounce serving (without butter, cream, or cheese, that is). It contains more vitamin C than orange juice. It is rich in minerals, indispensable for the bones and the skin. Choose cauliflower that is very white, without spots, heavy for its size, and with tight florets. It should be eaten as fresh as possible, but will hold 2 to 3 days in the vegetable drawer of your refrigerator. If it is cooked *au blanc* (in water with the addition of 2 tablespoons flour and the juice of ½ lemon), it will retain its color and will hardly smell at all.

It is often forgotten that cauliflower may be served raw, in little florets with vinaigrette or mayonnaise. In this way, it preserves all of its vitamins, which cooking partially destroys.

CREAM OF CAULIFLOWER SOUP
WITH MUSSELS

◆ ◆ ◆

Crème de chou-fleur aux moules

Serves 6 to 8

1 large cauliflower	1 large sprig of fresh thyme
1 tablespoon vinegar	or ½ teaspoon dried
6 cups light cream	1 small bay leaf
2 cups heavy cream	4 pounds mussels, cleaned
1 tablespoon butter	White pepper
2 medium-sized onions,	Salt
diced	1 teaspoon chopped fresh
1 tablespoon curry powder	chervil

Cut the cauliflower into 8 pieces. (Reserve several little florets to use as a garnish for the cooked soup.) Wash the cauliflower in water to which you have added the vinegar. Combine the creams and cauliflower in a large non-reactive saucepan, bring to a simmer, and cook over low heat for 20 minutes. Strain the cream without mashing or pressing down on the cauliflower. You do not want the cauliflower pulp to thicken the cream. Discard the cauliflower or use elsewhere.

In the meantime, heat the butter in a large flameproof casserole over moderate heat. Add the onions and sauté until soft but not browned. Add the curry powder, thyme, bay leaf, mussels, and freshly ground pepper to taste. Cover and cook over low heat until the mussels open. Let cool.

Shell the mussels, strain the cooking liquid, and add both to the cream. Stir over low heat without letting the mixture boil. Adjust the seasoning and ladle into warm soup bowls. Don't forget to garnish with the reserved florets and the chopped chervil. Serve immediately.

Wine: Alsatian Tokay (Pinot Gris)

CAULIFLOWER SALAD WITH SMOKED SALMON AND TOMATO SAUCE

◆ ◆ ◆

*Tartare de chou-fleur au saumon fumé
et au coulis de tomates*

Serves 4

½ medium-sized cauliflower
  (about ¾ pound)
2 tablespoons vinegar
Salt
½ pound smoked salmon
4 tablespoons mayonnaise
1 tablespoon ketchup
1 teaspoon Worcestershire
  sauce
Tabasco sauce

1½ tablespoons chopped
  chives
1 tablespoon lemon juice
6 small ripe tomatoes (about
  1½ pounds)
1 tablespoon tomato paste
⅔ cup olive oil
Pepper
1 small cabbage
1 tablespoon butter, melted

Wash the cauliflower in water to which you have added the vinegar. Boil in salted water until it is just tender. Drain and cool under cold running water. Drain well. Cut about a third of the smoked salmon in small dice and the remainder in long thin strips. Stir together the mayonnaise, ketchup, Worcestershire, and about ½ teaspoon Tabasco to make the "tartar" sauce.

Divide the cauliflower into florets and toss with the diced salmon and half the chives. Dress with the tartar sauce and lemon juice.

To make the *coulis*, core, peel, and seed the tomatoes and put in the blender with the tomato paste. Puree; then, with the motor running, gradually add the olive oil. Stir in salt, pepper, and Tabasco to taste.

Preheat the oven to 200° F.

Separate the leaves on the cabbage, wash, and cut out the thick central ribs. Bring a large pot of salted water to a boil. Add the cabbage leaves and boil for 2 minutes. Drain and dry on paper towels. Brush both sides of each leaf with melted butter. Lay these out in one layer on a baking sheet and bake for 30 minutes.

To serve, mound the cauliflower salad in the center of a serving platter. Decorate the top with a cross-hatch pattern of salmon strips. Pour the tomato *coulis* around the outside of the salad, arrange the cabbage leaves on the sauce, and garnish with the remaining chopped chives.

Wine: White Saint-Joseph

USING
YOUR NOODLE

◆ ◆ ◆

Who had the idea to start off with gruel,
to dry it out, to turn it into
flat cakes and then pasta?
This question will forever remain unanswered,
although pasta must surely count among
the very first preparations
that man conceived to feed himself.

◆◆◆◆◆◆◆◆◆◆◆◆◆◆◆◆◆◆◆◆◆◆◆◆◆◆◆◆◆◆◆◆◆◆◆◆◆

Evidence of pasta has been discovered in China, dating back to three millennia before Christ. It has been made of wheat flour, rice, corn, and even chick-pea flour. And if we reexamine the Old Testament, we find the Hebrews often speaking of flat cakes made of unleavened bread, without yeast. Doubtless they also made pasta. I do not, however, plan to get embroiled in this historical tangle—it truly is a labyrinth— but if you are interested in the subject I would suggest Martine Jolly's wonderful book *Le Monde des pâtes* (Robert Laffont).

Though I may disappoint some, I would recommend commercially made Italian pasta; those made by the Barilla and the De Cecco companies are both excellent. [*Both are available in the United States.*] Don't waste your time making it yourself. You'll have too much trouble finding the kind of hard semolina flour that's indispensable for high-quality pastas. Enjoy yourself making sauces to go on the pasta and take great care that it is correctly cooked.

The essential rule is to use a large pan, not made of a heavy material but rather of aluminum or stainless steel. You need about a gallon of water for each pound of pasta. Bring the water to a boil, then add about a tablespoon salt for each gallon and a little oil. Add the pasta and stir with a fork. Follow the cooking time indicated on the package and then drain well in a colander. Never rinse the pasta or let it sit in the cooking water because it will continue to absorb water. Toss with a little butter. Serve plain, with the sauce on the side, or with the sauce mixed in.

Cheeses that go best with pasta are mozzarella, Gorgonzola, French blue cheeses, pecorino, and, of course, Gruyère.

Pasta can be prepared in a thousand ways: from the most modest, simply tossed with some leftover roasting-pan juices or a little tomato-meat sauce, to the most sophisticated, garnished with strips of smoked salmon, caviar, diced foie gras, or truffles.

PESTO SAUCE

◆ ◆ ◆

Sauce pesto

Serves 4 to 6

30 large basil leaves
3 garlic cloves
½ cup grated pecorino
  Romano cheese
½ cup grated Parmesan
  cheese

½ cup pine nuts
About ½ cup olive oil
Salt

Chop the basil and garlic coarsely. Put them in a food processor or blender with both the cheeses and the pine nuts and grind until you have a smooth paste. You may need a little olive oil. Put this mixture in a bowl and gradually mix in the olive oil, stirring continuously until the sauce is creamy. Season with salt. Toss with about 1 pound cooked pasta.

MACARONI AND CHEESE

◆ ◆ ◆

Gratin de macaroni

This recipe is easy. You absolutely must try it.

Serves 2,
or 4 as a side dish

Salt
6 ounces (about 2 cups)
   macaroni
1½ cups heavy cream
3½ ounces Gruyère cheese
   (about 1 cup grated)

1½ ounces Parmesan cheese
   (about ½ cup grated)
Pinch of nutmeg
White pepper
1 egg yolk

Bring 8 cups salted water to a rapid boil. Add the macaroni and boil until it is just barely cooked through. Drain the pasta in a colander and keep shaking it until no water remains. Do not rinse it or cool it at this time. Put the macaroni in a baking dish and add the cream so that it covers the pasta. Cover and refrigerate overnight.

The following day, put the pasta in a colander over a bowl and allow to drain for a good 2 hours, stirring the macaroni around every so often. Set aside 2 tablespoons of the cream. Pour the remainder into a non-reactive saucepan, bring to a boil, remove from the heat, and stir in all but ¼ cup of the Gruyère, the Parmesan, and the nutmeg and season with salt and pepper to taste. Stir in the macaroni and spoon back into the baking dish.

Preheat the oven to 350° F.

Bake the macaroni in the oven for 15 to 20 minutes. Stir together the reserved 2 tablespoons cream with the egg yolk and the remaining ¼ cup Gruyère. Top the macaroni with this mixture and place under a preheated broiler until the top is bubbly and lightly browned.

You can eat the macaroni and cheese by itself or serve it as a side dish with any white meat such as roast veal or chicken.

Wine: White Côtes-du-Jura or white Arbois if you are going to eat the macaroni and cheese by itself

VERMICELLI WITH

BLACK CHINESE MUSHROOMS

◆ ◆ ◆

Vermicelles chinois aux champignons noirs

You can't talk about noodles without having at least one Chinese recipe.

Serves 2, or 4 as a side dish

3 ounces dried Chinese black mushrooms	1 large red bell pepper
½ pound Chinese vermicelli (thin wheat-flour noodles)	1 tablespoon butter
	1 small bunch chives
1 large green bell pepper	1½ tablespoons soy sauce (or more, to taste)

Soak the mushrooms for ½ hour in warm water. In the meantime, boil the noodles for about 3 minutes in rapidly boiling water, drain, and cool under cold running water. Drain well. Cut the peppers in half, remove the stems, seeds, and white ribs, and cut into thin julienne strips. Drain the mushrooms, cut off the stems and discard, and cut the caps into thin slices. Heat the butter in a skillet over moderate heat, add the peppers and mushrooms, and sauté until just softened. Add the noodles and continue cooking over low heat for 10 minutes. Cut the chives in 1-inch pieces. At the last moment, toss with the noodles, along with the soy sauce. Taste for seasoning and add more soy sauce if necessary.

You can serve the vermicelli as is, as a hot first course, but you could also serve it with pan-fried medallions of veal sweetbreads or chicken in cream sauce.

Wine: Chablis

SAINT BASIL

◆ ◆ ◆

A native of India, basil passed through Asia,
flourished in Egypt, and, four thousand years ago,
traveled to Greece and Italy,
finally gaining a foothold in northern Europe
by the sixteenth century.
It is impossible
to dissociate from Italian pesto
and Provençal pistou.

◆◆◆◆◆◆◆◆◆◆◆◆◆◆◆◆◆◆◆◆◆◆◆◆◆◆◆◆◆◆◆◆◆◆◆◆

A sacred plant in India, basil (*le basilic* in French) derived its name from the Greek *basilikon*, meaning "royal," which shows what secular prestige was once attached to the herb.

The flavor of its leaves is reminiscent of lemon and jasmine, but it loses its aroma when dried, to take on the flavor of mint. There exist several varieties, the best of which are agreeably spicy. It arouses and refreshes the mouth. It piques the appetite and acts as a tonic and antiseptic. Basil returns equilibrium to an upset stomach and calms nausea. At one time headaches were treated with basil oil. To make it, you need merely fill a bottle three-quarters full of the leaves, cover with oil, and let the basil macerate. If you do the same with vinegar, you will obtain excellent vinaigrettes. The combination of basil and tomato, which works wonders on our plates, is also found in the garden. In fact, basil protects tomatoes from parasites and diseases, and they seem to taste better when grown side by side. Basil attracts bees.

Its use in antiquity stirred up a certain amount of controversy. Some physicians said that it encouraged the reproduction of scorpions in the brain! Others asserted that it gave strength and courage and eliminated poisons from the body.

RAVIOLI WITH PESTO

◆ ◆ ◆

freezes well

Ravioli au pesto

Many stores that make fresh pasta will be happy to sell you fresh ready-made sheets of pasta dough. Otherwise, follow the recipe in the Appendix to make your own dough. Ravioli freezes well, so make an extra batch. Do not defrost the frozen ravioli before boiling. For the pesto, you can follow the recipe on page 212 or buy it ready-made.

Serves 4 to 6

1 medium-sized zucchini	2 egg yolks
1 celery stalk	3 shallots
½ small fennel bulb	1 medium-sized tomato
1 cup ricotta cheese	20 large basil leaves
7 tablespoons pesto	2 tablespoons white wine
Salt and white pepper	vinegar
1¼ pounds pasta dough in	⅓ cup dry white wine
sheets	¾ cup butter

Cut the zucchini, celery, and fennel into small dice (you should have about 2½ cups). Stir together these vegetables, the ricotta, and the pesto. Season with salt and pepper.

Mark half of the pasta sheets lightly into 2½- to 3-inch squares. Place about 1 tablespoon of the ricotta mixture in the center of each square. Brush the remaining sheets with the egg yolk on one side. Set these, egg side down, on top of the first sheets. Press down between each mound of filling so that it is well sealed in the dough. Cut apart into ravioli, once again making sure that each pasta pocket is entirely sealed in the dough.

Chop the shallots fine. Peel, seed, and dice the tomato. Chop the basil coarsely. Combine the shallots, vinegar, and wine in a small non-reactive saucepan over moderate heat. When the liquid is reduced to about 2 tablespoons, turn the heat down to low and gradually incorporate the butter, a small piece at a time, stirring continually. When the butter is almost entirely liquefied, remove from the heat and stir occasionally until all the butter has completely melted. Strain.

Bring a large pot of salted water to a boil. Add the ravioli and cook for 6 minutes. Drain carefully.

Mix the tomato and basil into the butter sauce. Season with salt and pepper. Pour the sauce over the ravioli and serve immediately.

Wine: White Châteauneuf-du-Pape, white Chignin

ROAST RACK OF LAMB WITH *PISTOU*

◆ ◆ ◆

Emincé d'agneau au pistou

The recipe asks you to use only the white (or red) ribs of the Swiss chard, not the whole leaf. Cut away the leaves and reserve for another purpose. (They are delicious sautéed slowly with a little olive oil and garlic.)

Serves 4

½ pound snow peas
½ pound green beans (*see note page 201*)
⅓ pound Swiss chard ribs
Salt
1 small bunch of parsley, with the stems removed
1 large bunch of chives
50 large fresh basil leaves
1¼ cups plus 2½ tablespoons softened butter

1 teaspoon mustard
1 tablespoon peanut oil
2 racks of lamb, each about 1¼ pounds
1 teaspoon thyme leaves
Pepper
1 medium-sized tomato
4 tablespoons heavy cream

Top and string the snow peas and beans. Cut the chard stems into 2-inch-by-¼-inch strips. Bring about 6 cups lightly salted water to a boil and separately cook each vegetable briefly: about 30 seconds for the snow peas, 2 to 3 minutes for the beans, and about 3 minutes for the chard. Drain and cool under cold running water.

Preheat the oven to 400° F.

Put the parsley, chives, and about three quarters of the basil in a food processor. Chop very fine. Add 1¼ cups of the butter and the mustard and puree. Set aside.

Set a roasting pan on top of the stove over moderately high heat. Add 1 tablespoon butter and the oil. When the fat is very hot, add the racks of lamb and brown well on all sides. Sprinkle with the thyme and season with salt and pepper to taste. Roast for 20 minutes or longer, depending on desired doneness. Remove from the oven and allow to rest for 15 minutes in a warm place.

Peel and seed the tomato and cut into ¼-inch dice. Chop the rest of the basil. Heat the remaining 1½ tablespoons butter in a skillet over moderate heat. Add the tomato, cook briefly, then add the vegetables and the chopped basil. Cook over low heat for about 10 minutes. Season with salt and pepper.

Pour the cream into a non-reactive saucepan over moderately low heat. When it is hot, just short of boiling, gradually incorporate the herb butter, spoonful by spoonful, stirring continually. Season with salt and pepper.

To serve, arrange the vegetables on a warm serving platter. Carve the lamb and mound it in the center of the vegetables. Spoon the sauce around the outside. Serve hot.

Wine: Red Saint-Joseph

◆◆◆◆◆◆◆◆◆◆◆◆◆◆◆◆◆◆◆◆◆◆◆◆◆◆◆◆◆◆◆◆◆◆◆◆

THE
GRAND FINALE

◆ ◆ ◆

*The table is cleared and
newly cleaned, and dessert appears.
It is when the meal comes to a full stop,
and you have an explosion of fireworks
conceived to surprise and enchant,
and to surpass all the delicacies that came before.*

◆◆◆◆◆◆◆◆◆◆◆◆◆◆◆◆◆◆◆◆◆◆◆◆◆◆◆◆◆◆◆◆◆◆◆◆◆◆

The generic term *dessert* encompasses cheeses as well as *entremets*. In the *grande cuisine classique*, this last term included vegetables, sweets, pastries, ice creams, and raw fruit, all served, in principle, after the cheese course.

The composition of the dessert used to be much more sumptuous. The great Marie-Antoine Carême even used to take architectural design classes to gain inspiration for his *pièces montées* (decorative centerpieces) and his pastries. These were supported by temples, porticoes, and pedestals, all of which really did make them the most brilliant part of the meal.

It was during the crusades that the French were introduced to sugar. This "spice" was derived from "reeds which gave off honey without the help of bees." First sold at exorbitant prices by apothecaries, sugar made possible the development of confectionery, candy, jams, and pastry. Until the Middle Ages, it was used to "season" meat and other savory dishes. The arrival of Catherine de Médicis in France in 1533 created a new style. Confectioners and pastry chefs made delicate *frangipane* (almond custard cream); soft macaroons; *gâteau de Milan*, or cream puff dough, which is said to have been created in 1540 by Popelini, chef to the queen.

Apicius had already invented honey-sweetened *crème renversée* (flan), in the year A.D. 25. However it is in 822, apparently, that we encounter the term *pâtisserie* for the first time, in a document from the court of Louis le Débonnaire (Louis I).

It was in the Neolithic Era that man first had the idea of placing a gruel of boiled cereals on a stone heated by the sun, giving us the first flat cake. Later, the Egyptians, the Greeks, the Romans, and the Gauls perfected the method by embellishing these cakes with poppy seeds, anise, fennel, or coriander. Traces of pudding and spice cakes can also be found in antiquity. Aristophanes mentions *melitunta*, made of sesame flour, eggs, and cheese and coated with honey after cooking. The Romans later added dried fruit and pepper.

RASPBERRIES AU GRATIN

WITH ALMOND CREAM

◆ ◆ ◆

Gratin de framboises à la crème d'amandes

Almond flour is available in specialty stores. A close approximation can be obtained by grinding ½ cup blanched almonds with the 4 tablespoons sugar in a food processor as fine as possible.

Serves 4

2 tablespoons softened butter	4 tablespoons sugar
½ cup almond flour	1 egg
	1½ pints raspberries

STRAWBERRY *COULIS*

1 cup strawberries	Lemon juice to taste
Sugar to taste	

Using a wooden spoon, stir together the butter, almond flour, and sugar until the mixture has a creamy consistency. Add the egg and stir until smooth. Set the raspberries in an ovenproof dish and cover with the almond mixture. Set under a preheated broiler and broil until golden.

To make the *coulis,* puree the strawberries in a blender or food processor. Add sugar and a little lemon juice to taste.

Spoon a ribbon of *coulis* over the warm raspberries and serve.

Accompany with a fruit *eau-de-vie* or a Muscat de Rivesaltes.

PEARS IN *FILO*

◆ ◆ ◆

Poires en croûte

Serves 4

6 pears	2 vanilla beans
10 tablespoons sugar	4–6 sheets *filo* dough
2 teaspoons lemon juice	⅓ cup melted butter

ALMOND PASTE

3 tablespoons softened butter	3 tablespoons sugar
6 tablespoons almond flour (*see note in preceding recipe*)	1 egg
	1½ tablespoons flour

SAUCE

14 tablespoons sugar	1¼ cups heavy cream
2½ tablespoons diced fresh ginger	10 tablespoons cocoa
	1 tablespoon butter

Peel the pears. Combine 4 cups water, the sugar, lemon juice, and vanilla beans in a saucepan over moderate heat. Bring to a boil and add the pears. Simmer for 5 minutes once the syrup has come to a boil. Pour off the syrup.

Make the almond paste: using a wooden spoon, stir together the butter, almond flour, and sugar until it has a creamy consistency. Add the egg and stir until smooth. Incorporate the flour.

Make the sauce: combine the sugar with ¼ cup water and the ginger in a heavy saucepan over moderate heat. When the sugar has melted and is beginning to turn golden, add the cream and simmer, stirring, until the sugar is dissolved. Stir in the cocoa. Pour into a blender and blend at high speed. Add the butter, in small pieces, and blend once more. Strain.

Core 4 of the pears and fill with the almond paste. Reserve the other 2 for decoration.

Spread out a sheet of the *filo* dough, brush lightly with the melted butter and set another piece on top. Cut out a piece of this double layer about 7 by 5 inches and wrap 1 pear in it. Take another sheet, butter it, and place another sheet on top. This time, cut the sheet into 1-inch strips. Take the wrapped pear and coil 2 of these strips—starting at the bottom and finishing at the top—in a spiral around the pear. Wrap the remaining stuffed pears in the same way.

Preheat the oven to 400° F.

Set the pears upright on a lightly buttered baking sheet. Set it on the stove over high heat for 20 seconds to heat the bottom, then set it in the preheated oven for 20 to 25 minutes.

Core the remaining pears and cut into thin strips. Fan these out along the edge of each plate. Set a warm baked pear in the center of each plate and spoon the chocolate sauce around it. You can also add a scoop of vanilla ice cream.

Wine: Banyuls

THE
CRÈME DE LA
CRÈME

◆ ◆ ◆

*Chiboust, located in Paris on the rue
Saint-Honoré, created a cake with the same
name in 1846. Thus, with his cream puffs,
he paid homage to his quarter, to his
patron saint, and to his guild.*

◆◆◆◆◆◆◆◆◆◆◆◆◆◆◆◆◆◆◆◆◆◆◆◆◆◆◆◆◆◆◆◆◆◆◆◆◆

The legend of Saint Honoré, Bishop of Amiens in the sixth century, recounts how one day, while celebrating Mass, he saw the Lord Himself come down to consecrate the Host. However, the saint didn't become popular in his native Picardy until the eleventh century, when, right after a procession the citizens of Amiens had held, bearing his reliquary, in order to end a drought, the rain began to fall. His renown spread quickly in Paris when Renaud Chérée and his wife, Sybille, transplanted from Picardy, built a handsome Gothic church in his honor. Parisians have remained faithful to the saint: witness the rue Saint-Honoré and the Faubourg-Saint-Honoré as well as the Church of Saint-Honoré-d'Eylau, which recalls the battle of that name (1807) in which, remarkably, the adversaries, Napoleon I and Alexander I of Russia, each convinced himself that he had won the battle.

Of course, when we speak of the Saint-Honoré of M. Chiboust, it is of a confection recognizable by its crown of cream puffs glazed with caramel. *Crème* Chiboust, which traditionally tops the Saint-Honoré, is a vanilla pastry cream lightened by the addition of beaten egg whites, incorporated while the mixture is still warm. For the sake of speed, you often find the Saint-Honoré simply topped with whipped cream.

GÂTEAU SAINT-HONORÉ

◆ ◆ ◆

You will need to buy puff pastry for this recipe. It is available frozen in specialty food stores and some supermarkets.

Serves 8

½ pound puff pastry   1 egg yolk

FOR THE *CHOUX* PASTRY

1 teaspoon salt   1¾ cups flour
7 tablespoons butter   5 eggs

FOR THE PASTRY CREAM

1 cup milk   5 tablespoons sugar
3 egg yolks   3½ tablespoons flour

FOR THE CARAMEL

14 tablespoons sugar

FOR THE WHIPPED CREAM

1 vanilla bean   1½ cups confectioners' sugar
3 cups heavy cream

Roll the puff pastry dough into an ⅛-inch-thick round. Cut out a 10-inch circle; set this on a baking sheet lined with parchment or very lightly buttered. Prick the center in several places with a fork. Place in the refrigerator.
Preheat the oven to 400° F.

To make the *choux* pastry, combine 1 cup and 2 tablespoons water, the salt, and the butter in a heavy saucepan over moderate heat. Bring to a boil and then, all at once, add the flour. Stir well with a wooden spoon until the dough no longer sticks to the sides of the pan. Remove from the heat and then stir in 1 egg at a time, making sure each egg is fully incorporated before adding the next. You could use a food processor or heavy-duty mixer to incorporate the eggs. Let the dough cool briefly.

Brush the puff pastry with a beaten egg yolk. Partially fill a pastry bag fitted with a ½-inch plain tip with the *choux* pastry and pipe a 1-inch-wide ring on the edge of the puff pastry circle. On another baking sheet, also lined with parchment or very lightly buttered, pipe about 20 balls of the *choux* dough, each about 1½ inches in diameter. Bake in the center of the oven: 20 minutes for the puffs and 25 minutes for the "crown."

In the meantime, prepare the pastry cream. Bring the milk to a boil. In a bowl, stir together the egg yolks, sugar, and flour. Gradually pour the hot milk into this mixture, stirring continually, then return all of this to the saucepan over moderately low heat. Cook, stirring continually, until the mixture is as thick as pudding. Do not let it boil. Let cool completely.

Make the caramel by combining the sugar with ¼ cup water in a heavy saucepan over moderately high heat. When the sugar has melted and turned a light golden brown, remove from the heat. Using a fork or a pair of tongs, carefully dip the puffs in the caramel and use the melted caramel to "glue" them to the edge of the crown.

Split the vanilla bean, scrape out the insides, and add these to the heavy cream along with the confectioners' sugar. Beat by hand or with an electric mixer until firm peaks form.

Fold one third of the whipped cream into the pastry cream and spread this in the center of the crown. Mound the rest of the whipped cream in a dome shape in the center, using a pastry bag fitted with a star tip.

RASPBERRY *GRATINS À LA CHIBOUST*

◆ ◆ ◆

Gratins de framboises à la Chiboust

Serves 8

RASPBERRY *COULIS*

2 pints (¾ pound)
raspberries

2 teaspoons lemon juice
2 tablespoons sugar

GRATINS

4 teaspoons (2 envelopes)
unflavored gelatin
9 tablespoons *crème fraîche*
8 egg yolks

3½ tablespoons flour
2 pints (¾ pound)
raspberries
Confectioners' sugar

ITALIAN MERINGUE

2 cups sugar

8 egg whites

You will need 8 ramekins, about 4 inches wide and a little over 1 inch deep.

Make the *coulis* by combining the raspberries and lemon juice in a food processor or blender. Blend until the raspberries are pureed but the seeds have not begun to break up. Strain. Set aside ¾ cup. Stir the sugar into the remainder and reserve.

Make the *gratins*: sprinkle the gelatin into ¼ cup cool water and let stand 10 minutes. Combine the ¾ cup unsweetened *coulis* with the *crème fraîche* in a non-reactive saucepan. Bring to a boil. In a bowl, whisk together the egg yolks and flour until smooth. Stir the hot cream mixture into the yolks, return to the saucepan, and cook over moderately low heat until thick and steaming. Do not allow to boil. Remove from the heat and whisk in the gelatin. Stir until the gelatin is completely dissolved. Pour this raspberry mixture into a bowl, cover, and set aside.

Make the meringue: in a saucepan, combine the sugar with ½ cup water, and bring to a boil over high heat. Cook until the syrup reaches 248° F. as measured on a candy thermometer, about 5 minutes. Beat the egg whites until soft peaks form. Whisk the hot syrup into the egg whites. Stir about one third of the whites into the raspberry *gratin* mixture, then fold in the rest. Using half of this mixture, spoon or pipe a layer of it in each ramekin, sprinkle with the fresh raspberries, and top with the remaining mixture. Smooth the tops. Refrigerate at least 1 hour, run a small knife around the inside edge of each ramekin, dip the outside briefly in hot water, and then unmold.

Preheat the oven to 325° F.

Powder the top of each *gratin* with the confectioners' sugar and set under a broiler very close to the flame or element, just long enough for the sugar to turn a golden brown. This should take no more than 20 seconds. Set in the preheated oven for 5 minutes, or until the edges begin to soften. Using a large spatula, carefully transfer the *gratins* to individual plates.

Serve immediately with the remaining *coulis* poured around each dessert.

Wine: Muscat de Rivesaltes

THE KINGS'
FOLLIES

◆ ◆ ◆

The New Year is upon us; the holidays are in full swing.
It is when our table becomes a land of milk and honey,
with cakes and pastries holding the place of honor.
Let us not forget tradition.
That of the galette des Rois
(the cake of the Three Kings)
is one of the most ancient.

◆◆

January is dedicated to Janus, the god with two faces, but also to gastronomy. It is, in fact, the month of family get-togethers, New Year's gifts, *marrons glacés* (candied chestnuts), and chocolate candy: toys and candy for the little ones, banquets good and bad for grownups. It is also the month of patron-saint feast days. The bakers honor their patron saint, following the holiday guide *L'Almanach de cocagne*, as do the butchers (Saint Anthony of the Desert), referred to by some as the feast of Saint-Cochon (literally, "Saint Pig"), and the wine makers (Saint Vincent). At the beginning of the century, the period between Christmas and Saint Anthony's Day was called *les semaines de cocagne*, the weeks of plenty.

We also have Epiphany, the feast of the Three Kings, Melchior, Gaspar, and Balthazar, who came to adore the Christ Child in Bethlehem, bringing myrrh, gold, and frankincense. Historically, this holiday is traced back to the Roman period. During the festivities honoring Saturn (the Saturnalia), all the rules of normal behavior were turned on their head; the people chose a "king for a day," drawing lots with the aid of a bean hidden in a flat cake. These pagan feast rites continued to exist under the Christian Church until the middle of the thirteenth century.

In the course of these *semaines de cocagne*, some very odd ceremonies were celebrated, known as the feasts of the lunatics, the fools, or the innocents. A bishop of the mad was elected —often a pauper—and dressed in all episcopal finery. Church dignitaries looked on as spectators, though some, as in Reims, became participants. The deacons and children of the choir dressed in the garments of the opposite sex, smeared their faces with soot, or wore grotesque masks. The altar was also made part of the revelry and utilized to serve *boudins* (blood sausages) and sausages. People drank out of the ciboria, while exchanging curses and blaspheming. Tradition also required old shoes to be burned so that their stench would be spread throughout the sacred edifice. These grotesque festivities took a long time to die out. It was not until the Middle Ages that the *gâteau des Rois* began to be associated with Epiphany. During the French Revolution, some patriots tried to replace it with a *gâteau de l'Egalité* or *de la Liberté* (the cake of Equality or of Liberty), but without success.

The carnival that begins on the day of Epiphany is a period of revelry that does not end until Lent. In France there are two great traditions for the *gâteau des Rois*. In the North, in Lyon and in the Paris region, there is a puff-pastry cake filled with almond cream, whereas in the South the people eat an enriched yeast cake scented with orange flower water or *eau-de-vie* and studded with candied fruit.

TART OF THE KINGS

◆ ◆ ◆

Galette des Rois

Serves 8

ALMOND PASTE

7 tablespoons softened
  butter
7 tablespoons sugar
14 tablespoons almond flour
  (*see note, page 226*)

2 eggs
2 tablespoons plus
  2 teaspoons flour

PASTRY CREAM

1 cup milk
4 tablespoons sugar

3 egg yolks
3½ tablespoons flour

2 dried fava beans
1½ pounds puff pastry (*see
note, page 232*)

1 egg yolk, beaten

Make the almond paste: beat the butter and sugar together
with a wooden spoon until light. Stir in the almond flour and
finally the eggs and flour.

Prepare the pastry cream: in a saucepan, bring the milk to
a boil. In a bowl, stir together the sugar, egg yolks, and flour.
Gradually pour the hot milk into this mixture, stirring continuously, then return all of this to the saucepan over moderately
low heat. Cook, stirring continuously, until the mixture is as
thick as pudding. Do not let it boil. Cool. Mix the pastry cream
with the almond paste and drop in the 2 beans.

Preheat the oven to 375° F.

Roll out the puff pastry into 2 rounds ⅛ inch thick and cut
out 2 circles each about 12 inches in diameter. Set one on a

baking sheet lined with parchment or very lightly buttered. Spread the pastry cream mixture on the puff pastry, leaving at least a ½-inch border. Brush this border lightly with water. Set the second sheet of pastry on top and crimp the edges well. Brush well with beaten egg yolk and then score the top in a crisscross design. Bake in the preheated oven for about 40 minutes, until golden. Serve warm.

Wine: A mellow, rich Vouvray

CAKE OF THE KINGS

◆ ◆ ◆

Gâteau des Rois

The traditional mix of candied fruit called for here includes melon, lemon, orange, and pineapple.

Serves 6

2¼ cups flour
1 teaspoon salt
1½ tablespoons sugar
3 whole eggs
Grated rind of 1 lemon
Grated rind of 1 orange
1 teaspoon orange flower
    water
7 tablespoons softened
    butter

¾ ounce fresh yeast or
    2 teaspoons active dry
    yeast
¾ cup mixed diced candied
    fruit
1 egg yolk, beaten
1 dried fava bean
Apricot jam

Combine the flour, salt, sugar, whole eggs, lemon rind, orange rind, orange flower water, butter, and a tablespoon water in a food processor. Process 10 seconds. Add the yeast and continue to process another 3 minutes, until the dough is smooth. Alternately, knead by hand. Turn the dough out onto a board and incorporate the candied fruit. Set in a bowl, cover with plastic wrap, and allow to rise in a warm place for 4 hours, or until doubled. Refrigerate the dough overnight.

Divide the dough into 6 equal pieces and form each in the shape of a ring, or "crown" (about 5 inches in diameter). Set these on baking sheets lined with parchment or very lightly buttered. Set in a warm oven (preheat to "warm" and then turn off the heat) to rise until doubled. Remove from the oven and brush with beaten egg yolk.

Preheat the oven to 350° F.

Bake the rings for 30 minutes. Remove from the oven. Turn one and only one of the cakes upside down, remove a piece of candied fruit, make a small hole, and insert 1 bean in the hole. Turn right side up and brush all the cakes with a little strained and warmed apricot jam.

Wine: Sauternes

AZTEC TREASURE

◆ ◆ ◆

For more than four centuries,
Europeans have considered chocolate
the supreme delicacy.
Its prehistory, however, is akin to myth.
The cacao bean conceals unsuspected riches
beneath its modest exterior.

◆◆◆◆◆◆◆◆◆◆◆◆◆◆◆◆◆◆◆◆◆◆◆◆◆◆◆◆◆◆◆◆◆◆◆◆◆

In a land of dreams there was once a garden. And in this garden there grew the largest and most beautiful tree of divine origin, the *cacahuaquchtl* (the cacao tree). The prophet gardener Quetzalcoatl, by eating the cacao beans, acquired the gift of universal knowledge—he became familiar with all human wisdom, and nature held no more secrets for him. But the gardener wanted to become immortal . . . A magician offered him a beverage that would fulfill this wish. Quetzalcoatl then went mad and the beautiful garden was destroyed.

For a long time, the Maya and the Aztecs sought to reclaim this era when the fruit of a tree could bring so much happiness. To console themselves, they used the cacao beans as coins; their unhappiness only increased. They yearned for the return of the plumed god, but it was Cortés who came, greedy for real gold, not for these beans masquerading as money.

At the time, the Aztecs were celebrating the festival of the new flame, the purifying flame that marked, in their calendar, the coming of a new century. They saw their hopes turned to an inferno, their civilization destroyed, while the Europeans began a new era not only by appropriating the Indians' gold but also by adopting their tomatoes, turkey, beans, and corn.

Was it folly or wisdom that chose this most bitter of beans to symbolize universal knowledge in the form of an undrinkable beverage? This is why the Christian religion, through the intervention of the nuns living in Oaxaca—convent life is predisposed to culinary research—thought to add sugar, cinnamon, and anise. In this way *xocoatl* received its patent of nobility and was accepted by the Old World.

CHOCOLATE TARTLETS

◆ ◆ ◆

Tartelettes au chocolat

Serves 6

PASTRY DOUGH

2¼ cups flour
1 cup confectioners' sugar
9 tablespoons butter

1 egg
1 pinch baking powder

CHOCOLATE CREAM

14 ounces bittersweet
  chocolate
9 tablespoons butter

1 teaspoon cinnamon
1 cup milk

Preheat the oven to 400° F.

Make the pastry dough: combine the flour, sugar, butter, egg, and baking powder in a food processor. Process until the dough forms a ball. Add a little water if necessary. Alternately, combine by hand. Roll out the dough ⅛ inch thick and cut out 6 (4-inch) circles. Lightly butter 6 small tart pans and line with the dough. Bake for about 8 minutes, or until golden. Let cool briefly and then unmold.

Make the chocolate cream: cut the chocolate and butter into small pieces and place in a bowl along with the cinnamon. Bring the milk to a boil and pour over the chocolate. Stir with a wooden spoon until the chocolate has melted and the mixture is smooth. Chill 1 hour.

Using an ice cream scoop or a small ladle, top the tarts with scoops of the chocolate mixture. Refrigerate 1½ hours before serving.

CHOCOLATE TRUFFLES

◆ ◆ ◆

Truffles au chocolat

Makes 16 to 20 truffles

¾ pound bittersweet chocolate
9 tablespoons *crème fraîche*

¼ teaspoon instant coffee
1 tablespoon dark rum
¾ cup cocoa

Break up the chocolate into small pieces. Put ½ pound in a bowl and set the rest aside. In a saucepan, combine the *crème fraîche* and coffee, bring to a boil, then pour into the bowl with the chocolate. Stir until the chocolate has melted and the mixture is smooth. Stir in the rum. Chill until thickened. Line a cookie sheet with parchment or wax paper. Using a pastry bag fitted with a large plain tip, pipe the chocolate mixture into ¾-inch balls on the paper. Refrigerate 1½ hours.

Put the remaining ¼ pound chocolate in a bowl and set over hot—not boiling—water. Stir until melted. Spread the cocoa in a flat bowl. Take the chocolate balls out of the refrigerator. With the help of a skewer, dip each in the melted chocolate and then roll in the cocoa. Chill. Serve the truffles at room temperature.

CHOCOLATE MOUSSE SQUARES
WITH *GIANDUJA*

◆ ◆ ◆

Croquant au gianduja

You will need Gianduja—*chocolate that has been mixed with ground roasted nuts—for this recipe. Chef Senderens mentions Fauchon in Paris as one likely source. In the United States, look for Perugina* Gianduia, *which is sold in the form of chocolate candy, or Belgian* Gianduja *(also known as* chocolat praliné*), sold in the form of chocolate bars.*

Serves 6

½ pound bittersweet
   chocolate
¾ pound *Gianduja*
3 tablespoons butter

1 cup heavy cream
1 recipe raspberry *coulis* (*see*
   page 234)

Break the chocolate into small pieces, put in a bowl, and set over hot—not boiling—water. Stir until melted. Spread the chocolate on a piece of parchment to a thickness of little more than ⅟₁₆ inch. When the chocolate is almost firm, cut into 18 equal-sized rectangles. Refrigerate.

Break the *Gianduja* into small pieces and melt in the same way as the chocolate. Incorporate the butter. Let cool briefly. Beat the cream until firm peaks form. Fold one third of the cream into the melted *Gianduja* and then fold in the remainder.

To assemble, spoon the chocolate mousse into a piping bag fitted with a large star tip. Pipe one twelfth of the mousse onto a rectangle of chocolate, add another layer of chocolate, another layer of mousse, and a final rectangle of chocolate. Repeat with the remainder.

Serve on a puddle of the raspberry *coulis*.

Is there a wine you can serve with chocolate?

The problem is caused by the intense taste of cocoa, the way it lingers on the palate, and the dominating character of its bitterness. There are certain wines, such as Banyuls, Maury, or an aged Rivesaltes, that are naturally sweet, with a full-bodied structure, so rich that they seem liqueur-like—in short, possessing a personality more powerful than chocolate itself. Their tonality is reminiscent of cocoa.

A FIG
FOR OUR TIME

◆ ◆ ◆

Along with grapes and walnuts,
figs arrive in their turn
among the fruits of autumn;
their flavors and colors bespeak the season.
Whether fresh or dried, white or purple,
the fig is much more than a delicious dessert.

◆◆

Figs, which originated in the Orient, like so many of our fruits, are now widespread throughout the Mediterranean area. Romans used to eat them with cooked ham and force-fed them to geese to fatten their livers (in French, *foie* [liver] and *figue* [fig] have the same etymological root). The Phoenicians, those great travelers, used to eat them dried on their sea expeditions and thus contributed to their wide dispersal. Elsewhere, the Corinthians used to cheat their Venetian buyers by mixing figs—which were cheaper—with raisins. This is where the French expression *mi-figue, mi-raisin* (meaning "neither one thing nor the other") originates.

Figs are a delicate fruit, available from the end of June through November. The firmness of the stem is a good indicator of freshness.

The dessert fruit *par excellence*, figs can be prepared in practically all the same ways as apricots; you can, however, also serve them with pork, duck, rabbit, or game. Cook them in the oven and then let them stew a few minutes in the roasting juices.

Here are four dessert recipes that will allow you to appreciate their flavor fully.

CARAMELIZED FIG TART

◆ ◆ ◆

Tarte aux figues caramélisées à la cannelle

Serves 6

½ pound puff pastry dough
(*see note, page 232*)
16 large fresh figs
1 tablespoon cinnamon

¼ teaspoon five-spice
powder (*see note, page 101*)
14 tablespoons light brown
sugar

Preheat the oven to 375° F.

Roll out the dough into a thin sheet, less than ⅛ inch thick. Cut this into 6 (6-inch) circles. Place these on a baking sheet lined with parchment or very lightly buttered. Take a cooling rack or similar grill and arrange it so that it rests about ½ inch above the dough. This will ensure that when the puff pastry rises, it will do so evenly. Bake about 20 minutes, until the pastry is puffed and golden.

Cut the figs in half and scoop out the flesh, leaving behind the white with the peel. Discard the peel. Lightly crush the fig flesh and stir in the cinnamon and five-spice powder. Spread the mixture on the tarts, mounding the fruit in the center.

Preheat the broiler.

Sprinkle the tarts with the brown sugar. Set under the broiler, about 3 or 4 inches away from the heat, and broil until the sugar has caramelized. Be careful the sugar does not burn. Serve immediately.

ROAST FIGS WITH RASPBERRIES

◆ ◆ ◆

Figues rôties aux framboises
et coulis de framboises

Serves 4

12 large fresh figs
3 tablespoons melted butter
3 tablespoons sugar

½ pint raspberries
1 ½ cups raspberry *coulis* (*see page 234*)

Preheat the oven to 375° F.

Cut off the stem of each fig, set the figs in a baking dish, brush them with the butter, and sprinkle with the sugar. Set in the oven and bake 15 minutes, until they are lightly caramelized.

Remove from the oven. With a pair of scissors, make a cross-shaped incision in the top of each fig so that you can open them like a flower.

Arrange 3 figs on each plate and garnish the center of each with a few raspberries. Spoon the *coulis* around the figs.

POACHED FIGS WITH

CHOCOLATE SAUCE

◆ ◆ ◆

Figues pochées sauce chocolat

Serves 4

1 orange
14 tablespoons sugar
2-inch piece of cinnamon

½ vanilla bean
12 large fresh figs

CHOCOLATE SAUCE

7 tablespoons cocoa   1½ tablespoons butter
¾ cup sugar

Using a vegetable peeler, remove the rind of the orange. In a saucepan, combine the rind, sugar, cinnamon, vanilla bean, and 4 cups water. Bring to a boil and simmer for 10 minutes. Let cool completely. Add the figs to the syrup and bring once more to a boil, remove from the heat, and let the figs cool to room temperature in the syrup.

In the meantime, make the chocolate sauce: combine the cocoa and sugar. Stir in 1 cup boiling water and then stir in the butter.

Drain the figs, set 3 warm figs in the middle of each plate, and spoon the warm sauce over them. Serve immediately.

You can also serve the figs with a scoop of vanilla ice cream in the center of each plate. Alternatively, you can sprinkle the figs with strips of candied orange peel or candied ginger.

FIGS WITH RASPBERRY CREAM

◆ ◆ ◆

Figues à la mousse de framboise

Serves 4

1 pint raspberries   ¾ cup heavy cream
½ cup confectioners' sugar   12 ripe white figs

Puree the raspberries in a blender or food processor. Press through a fine sieve to remove the seeds; stir in half the sugar. Whip the cream and the remaining sugar until stiff. Fold the raspberry puree into the whipped cream.

Peel the figs and cut in quarters. Put the figs in individual dishes and cover with the raspberry mousse. Refrigerate ½ hour before serving.

FORBIDDING
FRUIT

◆ ◆ ◆

The forbidden fruit of biblical tradition.
The most widely consumed fruit in France,
which has become the world's premier producer.
Our concern here is not the apple of discord
but, rather, a flavorsome morsel
that will know how to seduce you.

In his book *A la fortune du pot* ("Potluck")—a must-read for all those who have an interest in gastronomy—Mathias Lair destroys the legend that the apple was the forbidden fruit of the Bible. The author explains how *fructus*, in Latin, means "product, yield, gain," and thus the reference is not originally alimentary; the forbidden fruit is simply that which comes from the tree of knowledge, and thus it never was the apple. It is an error of translation! In fact, according to Mathias Lair, the word for fruit is *pomum*, and for the first Roman and later the Gallic translators of the Bible, the apple was the fruit *par excellence*. Moreover, *malum* (apple, in Latin) also, through an accident of language, designated badness, malfeasance, fault. It is thus that we see "apple" where "fruit" should be inscribed . . . So, ladies and gentlemen, bite into an apple—it is no longer forbidden.

It is estimated that in antiquity there were some thirty varieties of apple. In the sixteenth century, the count had risen to eleven hundred. In 1989, they numbered six thousand.

In France, Golden Delicious apples represent almost two thirds of all production; Granny Smiths, 12 percent; Red Delicious, 10 percent; all the others, 14 percent.

Apples are excellent at satisfying hunger and contain few calories (50 for each 3½-ounce serving). The following is a list of some outstanding apples, with their optimal seasons and characteristics.

—*Reine des reinettes:* October through March; striated with yellow and red, the flesh delicate and juicy
—Starking: January through April; red, tart, and crisp
—Golden Delicious: December through February; yellow, sweet, with delicate flesh
—Cox's: October through January; pale yellow striated with red, crisp and aromatic
—Calville: November through February; pale yellow, very delicate, one of the best
—*Reinette grise du Canada:* October through February; irregular and wrinkled, the flesh juicy and tart
—*Reinette blanche d'Auvergne:* January through May; large and irregular, delicate and juicy
—Melrose: September through April; red, sweet, and aromatic
—Clochard: October through April; yellowish green, delicate, and quite juicy
—*Belle de Boskoop:* December through March; large, with thick skin, sweet and perfumed

(Many of these varieties are not grown in the United States, though you may encounter analogous varieties cultivated by specialized growers. Farmer's markets are an especially good source.)

APPLE CAKE

WITH CUSTARD SAUCE

◆ ◆ ◆

Gâteau de pommes sauce anglaise

Make sure to use apples such as Granny Smith, Northern Spy, Winesap, or Red Delicious, which do not fall apart in cooking.

Serves 4

⅔ cup milk   2 pounds apples
2 egg yolks   7 tablespoons butter
13 tablespoons sugar   1½ teaspoons cinnamon

Bring the milk to a boil. Stir the egg yolks together with 3 tablespoons of the sugar, then gradually stir in the hot milk. Pour into a small non-reactive saucepan and set over low heat. Cook, stirring, until the sauce is thick enough to cover the back of a spoon. Set aside to cool. Cover and refrigerate.

Preheat the oven to 425° F.

Peel and core the apples, then slice very thin. Butter an ovenproof ceramic mold 5 inches round by 2 inches deep with 1 tablespoon of the butter (the mold must be shallow; if it is smaller, you may need fewer apples). Sprinkle all over with 2 tablespoons of the sugar. Melt the remaining butter.

Line the sides of the mold with about a third of the apples. Sprinkle with a third each of the remaining sugar and butter and the cinnamon. Spread another third of the apples flat in the mold, pressing them down. Sprinkle once more with a third of the sugar, butter, and cinnamon. Spread the remaining apples and finish with the remaining sugar, butter, and cinnamon.

Bake in the preheated oven for about 40 minutes. When the apples are cooked through, remove from the oven and let cool briefly. Unmold while still warm: place the serving plate on top of the cake and turn the mold upside down, carefully removing the mold. Serve the cake warm: spoon a pool of the cold custard sauce on each plate and top with a slice of the cake.

CARAMELIZED APPLES

◆ ◆ ◆

Pommes caramélisées

Serves 6

2 cups milk	3 tablespoons butter
6 egg yolks	¾ cup pine nuts, coarsely
1 cup plus 7 tablespoons	chopped
sugar	
4 Golden Delicious or	
Russet apples	

Prepare the custard sauce as in the preceding recipe, using the milk, egg yolks, and 7 tablespoons sugar. Set aside to cool. Cover and refrigerate.

Peel the apples, cut each into 6 pieces, and cut out the core. Sprinkle lightly with sugar. Heat the butter in a large skillet over moderately high heat. When the butter just begins to turn brown, add the apples. Cook briefly to brown lightly on all sides.

Combine the remaining sugar and about ¼ cup water in a heavy, medium-sized saucepan over moderate heat. Cook until the sugar begins to turn to a golden caramel. Dip each piece of apple in the caramel, roll in the pine nuts, then finally dip for 2 seconds in ice water. Let dry briefly on a clean, lint-free kitchen towel. Serve immediately.

To serve, spoon the custard sauce around the bottom of each plate and set the warm apples on top.

You could also substitute sesame seeds for the pine nuts.

GRATED APPLE TART

◆ ◆ ◆

Tarte aux pommes râpées

Serves 6

½ recipe pastry dough (*pâte brisée*) (*see Appendix*)

6 apples

4 tablespoons light brown sugar

4 tablespoons almond flour (*see note, page 226*)

1 tablespoon dark rum

12 tablespoons cinnamon

Preheat the oven to 400° F.

Roll out the dough to about ⅛-inch thickness and with it line a 12-inch tart pan. Line with aluminum foil and fill with dried beans or pie weights. Bake for 15 minutes. Remove the foil and weights and let cool.

Peel, core, and coarsely grate the apples. Stir in the sugar, almond flour, rum, and cinnamon. Spoon this mixture into the pie shell and bake at 350° F. for about 45 minutes, or until golden. Serve warm or at room temperature.

APPLE SORBET

◆ ◆ ◆

Sorbet aux pommes

Serves 6

4 cups fresh apple cider

Juice of 2 lemons

6 tablespoons Calvados

1¼ cups sugar

1 egg white

Stir together all the ingredients until the sugar is completely dissolved. Freeze in an ice cream maker, following the manufacturer's directions.

The best beverage to serve with these apple-based desserts is hard cider, Calvados, or another apple *eau-de-vie*.

ISLES OF
SWEETNESS

◆ ◆ ◆

Rum, coconut, pineapple . . .
they give us a foretaste of paradise,
and a base for our dessert,
our piñacolada sauce.
Far from the swaying palms,
open your mouth, close your eyes,
and France becomes an island . . .

In October of 1492, Christopher Columbus, having set out on his Western voyage of discovery, sighted land and first made landfall on the island of San Salvador, in what is now the Bahamas. He then went on to Cuba, which he baptized Juana. What amazed Columbus and his men the most in this unknown universe was one particular native custom: they give off smoke, he wrote in his journal, which is to say that they smoke the rolled leaves of a plant cultivated on the island and called *cohiba*. This generic name has become a trademark for a cigar company, Fidel Castro's favorite brand.

In exchange for this plant and the secret of its curing, Columbus gave the Taino Indians sugarcane, which he had brought along with the provisions necessary for this extraordinary expedition. The cane grew quickly in this region and established itself with great success—it germinated in seven days. Sugar wine, which was to become rum, was only "discovered" sometime between 1640 and 1694. As with Champagne, it was a member of a religious order who finally succeeded—it took eleven years!—to civilize this "alcohol of the savages" and to transform it into *eau-de-vie*. But in fact Marco

Polo had already spoken of such a "fire water" when he dictated his memoirs in a Genoese prison. It should be emphasized that distilled alcohol as well as the words *alcohol* and *alembic* are Arabic in origin and long predate this era.

Having made landfall in Cuba, Columbus set off for Guadeloupe and discovered the pineapple. The Spaniards thought this new fruit resembled a pine cone, which is where the Spanish *piña* originates, as well as the English *pineapple*. I will have nothing to do with those who claim that the pineapple first appeared in the twelfth century in Brazil! Know only that it is not advisable to keep a pineapple refrigerated, since the fruit dislikes temperatures that dip below 45° F.

The coconut, used since time immemorial in Southeast Asia and Polynesia, was discovered by Marco Polo, who called it the nut of Pharaoh. Coconut milk, made by grating the white flesh of the ripe coconut (not to be confused with coconut water, the liquid the nut contains), is highly prized in Indian cooking, especially in curry sauces and in the cooking of rice. In Polynesia, it is used for fish marinades. During a trip to the Antilles I was won over by the piñacolada: ⅓ rum, ⅓ coconut milk, ⅓ pineapple juice, mixed and, most important, shaken well. On my return to Paris I hastened to make a *sauce anglaise* with coconut milk and a complete dessert that would show off my pineapple fritters.

PINEAPPLE FRITTERS
WITH PIÑACOLADA SAUCE

◆ ◆ ◆

Beignets d'ananas à la piñacolada

The coconut milk called for here is available canned in any grocery that caters to immigrants from Southeast Asia. You can also substitute sweetened cream of coconut, which is available in most supermarkets. In that case, omit the sugar.

Serves 8

SORBET

1 cup sugar   2 cups pineapple juice

SAUCE

1½ cups coconut milk   5 tablespoons sugar
1 cup pineapple juice   2 tablespoons rum
8 egg yolks

FRITTERS

1 cup beer   6 (½-inch) slices fresh
1 tablespoon active dry yeast   pineapple
1 cup flour   3 cups peanut oil

Prepare the sorbet several hours in advance. Combine the sugar and 1 cup water in a saucepan and bring to a boil. Mix with the pineapple juice and chill. Freeze in an ice cream maker, following the manufacturer's directions.

Make the sauce: combine the coconut milk and pineapple juice in a non-reactive saucepan. Heat until just barely simmering. Stir together the egg yolks, sugar, and rum, then gradually stir in the hot coconut milk mixture. Return to the saucepan and set over low heat. Cook, stirring, until the sauce is thick enough to cover the back of a spoon. Set aside to cool. Cover and refrigerate.

Make the fritters: stir together the beer and the yeast. Mix in the flour and allow to rest for 20 minutes at room temperature.

Cut away the rind from the pineapple slices and cut out the tough central core. Cut each slice into 4 pieces. Blot them dry on paper towels.

Heat the oil in a heavy saucepan over moderate heat. When the oil is hot, about 370° F., use a fork to dip each piece of pineapple in the batter and then place it in the hot oil. Fry about 3 minutes on each side. Use a slotted spoon to remove the fritters and then drain on paper towels.

To serve, cover the bottom of each plate with sauce. Place a scoop of the pineapple sorbet in the center and then arrange three hot fritters in a circle around it.

This dessert cries out for the company of a fine white rum, such as the Trois Rivières rum, redolent of exotic perfumes. Fiery and powerful, this rum is nevertheless remarkably fruity, with the aromas of mangoes and pineapples, which give way to a note of vanilla. It is obtained by the distillation of pure sugarcane juices on the Trois Rivières plantations, the sunniest on the island of Saint Lucia.

Of all the hard alcohols, rum conserves best the flavor of the original product from which it is distilled. The distillates derived from a starch base, such as vodka (made from potatoes), or gin and whiskey (made from various cereals), have to be either cooked or malted. In the case of rum, made directly from sugar, it's unnecessary to transform starch into sugar. Rum, therefore, in contrast to gin or vodka, does not need to be "forced." It is the alcohol that undergoes the fewest chemical procedures. Rum can be aged in used barrels because it doesn't need the tannin that new barrels impart to other distillates, such as Armagnac and Cognac.

THE RED
AND THE WHITE

◆ ◆ ◆

*The power and finesse of its perfume
enveloped in floral tones:
Châteauneuf-du-Pape
is a wine touched by the divine.
In harmony with red mullet and
black olives, it is sublime.*

◆◆

The *château neuf* ("new castle"), today a ruin, was once the summer residence of the Avignon Popes. It was John XXII, in the fourteenth century, who had vines planted in his pleasure gardens. This appellation, now best known for its red wine, originally used to produce primarily white. The restoration of this papal color is due to some dozen dark years when the reds languished in popularity. Thus it is that white Châteauneuf-du-Pape, which used to be little more than a curiosity, has become a wine that is now highly in demand. I like it a great deal, especially the 1986 Beaucastel produced by Jean-Pierre Perrin. It is rich in flavor, with hints of linden blossoms, broom, bitter almond, and a touch of the exotic.

You will need to seek a companion for this young lady that will elicit a sunny harmony, and that will be able to seduce the rounded flesh of this divine bottle, with its somewhat weighty texture, recalling the earth where she was born. Who better than the red mullet? Even if he does come from the North.

RED MULLET
À LA CALABRAISE

◆ ◆ ◆

Rougets à la calabraise

Red mullet, rouget barbet or rouget de roche in French, is a highly prized rock fish with sweet flesh and red skin. It is virtually impossible to obtain in the United States. The best alternative is to substitute the fillets from 4 small red snappers for the red mullet fillets, making sure to reserve the livers for the croutons. You could omit the croutons if this proves impractical.

Serves 4

1 large fennel bulb
Salt
1½ cups olive oil
¼ pound black Niçoise
  olives
1 large garlic clove
8 red mullet livers
2 teaspoons pine nuts
2 anchovy fillets
1 thin slice white bread
½ lemon
1 teaspoon wine vinegar

1 teaspoon sherry vinegar
3 tablespoons peanut oil
Pepper to taste
¼ pound *mâche*
Fillets from 8 red mullets
½ teaspoon dried marjoram
5 tablespoons butter
1 tablespoon capers
1 tablespoon sliced pitted
  green olives
1 tablespoon chopped Italian
  parsley

Begin by cooking the fennel. Trim and wash the bulb, then boil in lightly salted water for 10 minutes. Cool under cold running water and drain well. Place it in a small baking dish, add 1 cup of the olive oil, cover, set your oven at 200° F. and bake for 3 hours.

Make a *tapenade*: pit the black olives and chop very fine. Chop the garlic fine. Heat ¼ cup of the olive oil in a small skillet over low heat. Add the garlic and cook briefly, without letting it color. Add the chopped olives and cook, uncovered, over very low heat for 1 hour, stirring occasionally.

Heat 1 teaspoon olive oil in a small skillet over moderate heat. Add the fish livers and sauté until they are cooked through. Let cool. Chop the pine nuts fine in a food processor or mortar, add the anchovies and livers, and puree. Press through a coarse sieve. Using a cookie cutter, cut 4 (1-inch) rounds out of the bread. Toast, cool, and then top the little toast circles with the liver mixture, using a teaspoon to smooth each into a little dome.

Peel the yellow zest of the half lemon with a vegetable peeler. Slice the zest into extremely thin strips. Place these in a small saucepan, cover with cold water, bring to a boil, and cook for 2 minutes. Drain and cool under cold running water.

Prepare the vinaigrette by stirring together the 2 vinegars and the peanut oil. Season with salt and pepper.

Cut the fennel into 16 little wedges. Season with salt and pepper. Heat the fennel, croutons, and *tapenade* in a 275° F. oven, keeping them separate. Toss the *mâche* with the vinaigrette and garnish the top of each plate with a mound of the salad.

Heat 1 tablespoon olive oil in a large skillet over moderately high heat. Add the fish fillets and cook until they are just barely cooked through: about 2 minutes on the skin side and 1 minute on the other side. Season with salt and marjoram.

Heat the butter in a skillet over moderately high heat. Season with salt and pepper. When the butter foams, add the lemon zest, capers, green olives, parsley, and about 1 teaspoon lemon juice. Taste for seasoning.

Arrange 2 red snapper (or 4 red mullet) fillets on each plate, across from the *mâche*. Place 4 pieces of fennel between them and a small scoop of *tapenade* on either side of the *mâche*. Set a crouton in the center of the plate. Spoon the seasoned butter over each fillet. Serve with Olive Bread (recipe follows).

Wine: White Châteauneuf-du-Pape, Château de Beaucastel

OLIVE BREAD

◆ ◆ ◆

Pain aux olives

Chef Senderens suggests that you go to your local bakery and buy some bread dough. Though this is unlikely to be practical in most North American cities, you will find that most pizzerias will be perfectly happy to sell you pizza dough—which is more or less the same thing. You can also make your own, of course.

Serves 4

½ cup chopped black   ½ pound bread dough
   Niçoise olives   Olive oil

Work the olives into the bread dough, cover, and refrigerate overnight. The following day, divide the dough in 4 and form each piece into a long cylinder, like a little *baguette*. Set on a baking sheet, cover, and let rise about 1 hour at room temperature.

Preheat the oven to 450° F.

Make 4 diagonal incisions in the top of each loaf with a razor blade. Brush lightly with olive oil. Bake for 8 to 10 minutes. Serve warm.

◆◆◆◆◆◆◆◆◆◆◆◆◆◆◆◆◆◆◆◆◆◆◆◆◆◆◆◆◆◆◆◆◆◆◆◆

THE WINE
AND THE CELLAR

◆ ◆ ◆

In terms of space, coolness, and absence of light,
your wine deserves an environment
where it can lead a quiet life
until the moment when it is to be served.
Always make sure to drink
each bottle at the appropriate temperature.

◆◆

"It is the cellar that makes the wine," goes an old saying.

The ideal temperature for a wine cellar is between 48° and 54° F. It is absolutely essential to avoid large swings in temperature. The environment cannot be too dry or too humid—it should read 70 percent on a hygrometer—so as to avoid the corks' drying out. Arrange for gentle ventilation and as little light as possible, since with bright light there is the risk of oxidization. Ideally, the room should be located belowground, with a floor of beaten earth, covered with gravel or flagstones. Above all, do not make the floor out of cement. You also have to ensure that the cellar is free of vibration and noise, and free of the slightest odor (such as that of fuel oil or cheeses) that might by absorbed by the wine.

The bottles must remain horizontal in the rack. The wine needs to remain in contact with the cork, so that the cork does not dry out and let in air and, with it, all kinds of germs harmful to the wine.

ENTER THE WINE

You need to bring the wine from cellar temperature to serving temperature gradually. It is better, all things considered, to serve a wine too cold than too warm, since once it is served, it will warm up in the glass. It used to be that serving wine "at room temperature" meant simply that: serving it at the ambient temperature of the room. What does "at room temperature" mean today? Wine experts, both in France and abroad, consider a temperature of 60° to 62° F. to correspond to the average dining room temperature in times past, and advise that red wines should not be served warmer than this; otherwise they lose their "bite."

Here is a basic guide to appropriate serving temperatures:

Champagne: 42° to 46° F.
Sweet white wines: 46° F.
Dry white wines: 46° to 50° F.

Avoid chilling white wine by placing it in the freezer or by immersing it in a wine bucket filled with ice and rock salt. Both, in lowering the temperature so quickly, have a tendency to "break" the wine.

Red Burgundy: 57° to 61° F.
Red Bordeaux: 59° to 61° F.
Red Rhône: 59° to 61° F.
Red Loire: 57° to 59° F.
Light red wine to be served chilled: 50° to 54° F.
Full-bodied, robust wine: 57° F.

When you serve red wine at room temperature, do not set it down near a heat source, which will raise the temperature of the wine too quickly and thus cause it harm.

OPENING AND DECANTING

Before uncorking the bottle, remove the lead capsule to just below the collar. The wine should not come in contact with the metal of the capsule. In theory, the cork should not be pierced all the way through to the bottom. Once you have removed it, smell it. There should be no fungal odor, nor should it smell of the cork (the wine should not smell "corky"). Finally, just to make sure, taste the wine before you serve it to your companions.

When should you open the bottle? Should it be a long time before it is to be served? It is a question that needs to be asked. It all depends on the age and quality of the wine. Young wines tend to improve a little when they are opened several hours in advance. They may even gain some of the suppleness that their vigor overwhelms. On the other hand, great wines of a certain age have more to lose than to gain. Open them too early, and there is the risk that their bouquet may fade. Too late, and there is every chance that they'll be marvelous—but only with the last swallow. It does appear that decanting is sometimes beneficial when there is sediment at the bottom of the bottle. In this case, the wine is carefully poured into a carafe, leaving the solid particles behind. Wines that are very young and robust can also be decanted in order to aerate them and facilitate favorable oxidization. When a wine is very fragile and old, it requires a great deal of care. Go to the cellar and place it lovingly in a basket in exactly the same position it occupied on the rack. With Burgundies, which are susceptible to oxidization and less tannic than Bordeaux, decanting may prove harmful. Only the nature of the wine will dictate whether it should be decanted and at what moment. Some old Bordeaux open up only after two or three hours, by which time others will have already begun to lose their bouquet. If there is doubt, it is better to decant a wine at the last moment. It will always be able to open up in your glass. In general, you should decant wines from the really great years and leave those from the lesser years alone. If you should have the misfortune to un-cork a bad bottle, you can use it for cooking, or make it into vinegar or mulled wine. Do not throw out these bad uncorked bottles; you may also be able to get a refund from your wine merchant.

THE HOLY
TRINITY

◆ ◆ ◆

If man had only three foods on which to live,
they could certainly be bread, wine, and cheese.
They are fundamental to our cuisine
and act as essential symbols.
Yet it isn't always clear how to
match one with the others.

The trio made up of bread, wine, and cheese has an important place in our culture, not only culinary but also symbolic. These three glorious fermentations are, in fact, the foods onto which most of our myths are grafted.

BREAD AS SYMBOL

Bread, before it became a Christian emblem, was full of pagan symbolism. Churches were often built on pagan sites, so that the people would keep coming to these places. And, often, the same symbols were retained, though the meaning might be changed. Thus we have come to have some very "sexual" bread names, such as *miches* ("buttocks") for round loaves of bread. In the Southwest of France, there is a bread in the form of a double phallus called *deux-noeuds* ("two knots"). In Italy, you find "angel pricks" and in England and the United States, "buns"—like the slang name for buttocks. The French word *four* ("oven") comes from the Church Latin *fornicatio*, which is derived from *fornis* ("vault") and by extension signifies "prostitute." This is because in Rome these women used to ply their trade in vaulted rooms.

Similarly, in ancient tradition long before Christ and the Last Supper, the vine was symbolically identified with the Tree of Life in paradise. The vine, in "producing" wine, is the metaphor for knowledge. Milk is the quintessential representation of spiritual food; to ponder milk is to ponder science or knowledge. Wheat, vines, and milk were thus magnified by the human spirit.

Matching wine and cheese is not always straightforward or easy. The intervention of the third interloper is necessary in order to make the connection and to eliminate any serious discord. You need bread. The grammar of French gastronomy is based on the usage of wine; conjugating it correctly is more arduous and more fraught with error than conjugating French verbs. It takes work, since unfortunate, painful, and sad combinations are legion. There are certainly cheeses that do go with red wine, but those that are enhanced by white wine are more numerous, and this combination is often more judicious. Finally, there are limited cases in which only *eau-de-vie* will make for a happy moment.

TIME FOR CHEESE

When, at the end of the meal, the cheese arrives on the table, a difficult choice must be made, and this is often poorly done. Food means something different to each one of us; we see it through the individual prism of our memory. Some foods speak to us in gentle tones, whereas others elicit fear. We all have our likes and dislikes. They are often just a question of habit, which has its reasons—having nothing to do with reason. The liquids and solids we ingest day after day do maintain our bodies but they should engage our consciousness, so that we don't waste our precious resources; thus we can transform this daily act into a legitimate defense. Wine must be "spelled out," drop by drop, to be understood, since to comprehend is to absorb, to take into oneself. Food desires that its quintessence is not merely used to renew our cells but that it should also furnish us with a supplement of aesthetic energy; and in order to do that, it must battle against the essential complacency of man—the quality that makes him say, "All tastes are a function of nature, but my taste is the best." There is, however, a difference between the taste which attracts us to things and the taste (the knowledge) that makes us know and discern quality and its absence.

In this green field of the aesthetics of taste, which goes against the sediments of history (or of habit) buried beneath it, our individuality triumphs and we take charge of ourselves. For some it is a tragic loss through the disintegration of tradition; for others it is progress. Each possesses his own "taste," but perhaps I may be allowed a few suggestions for those who continue to chew in the dark.

THE STAGING

It is up to you to arrange the food and wine—the actors—so that each, in his scene, will take on his particular role. And perhaps now it will be clear to you that you have often not shown them to best advantage. The goal is to be able to choose freely, through comparison and learning, until you have gained some objectivity in a field where subjectivity has held sway. The rule is to "play" fairly, being aware that what is pleasing to one person is not necessarily so to another. But don't forget that sensitivity to the four flavors—sweet, bitter, sour, and salty—differs from person to person.

BLISSFUL
UNIONS

◆ ◆ ◆

To taste wine together with bread and cheese
is to play a game with multiple combinations:
an interplay of volume and density
in your mouth in which you will discover
subtle nuances as the seasons unfold.

◆◆

Let's begin by setting practical rules for tasting: smell the wine and then taste it until it is imprinted on your memory. Now taste the cheese and then, finally, the bread, in order to remove the fattiness of the cheese. Now taste the wine once again. And that's how it all begins: do they go together, or do they not? Try tasting a second time without the bread if you need to be convinced of its importance in this exercise. You will see the difference, especially with very fatty cheeses; less so with dry cheeses and those made with scalded curds. In general, serve a lightly toasted white country-style bread with all cheeses. But if you wish to go further in your search for just the right match, know that soft cheeses with a washed alkaline rind—such as Epoisses and Maroilles—will need bread containing at least one third rye flour. With Munster, serve this same bread with a hint of cumin. Goat and blue cheeses require bread with nuts and raisins. But above all (to my taste), omit butter.

As I write these lines, it occurs to me to try some bread and olives (or olive bread) with a goat cheese (*chèvre*) from the Ardèche and a white Saint-Joseph. I'll leave it to you to try it out! If you should make a great discovery, share it with me.

RED?

Let's begin with the convention of red wine. I have always wondered whence the inseparable bonds between red wine and cheese derived their legitimacy. Nevertheless, it is the case that hard cheeses are generally better with red wine, that the flavor of a young wine with active tannin will be improved by a young cheese, and that a well-aged cheese will seek out an abundance of tannin.

Common wisdom has it that a cheese from one region will marry well only with a cheese from the same area. You'll see that there are numerous exceptions to this so-called rule. A Brie de Meaux and the wines from the Coteaux Champenois seldom get along; an old white Burgundy or a red Pernand-Vergelesses, however, make for a much more blissful union. The encounter of a Saint-Nectaire with a red Bordeaux might be of some interest, but it will hardly be love at first sight. Often a Saint-Emilion is suggested, whereas a red Graves would be better able to hold up a conversation and a white Châteauneuf-du-Pape would be positively seductive. Camembert (depending on the degree of ripeness, as with all cheeses) is content with hard cider, either sweet or dry, depending on your sweet-savory threshold. However, the common combination of Camembert with Beaujolais, which some seem to find inseparably riveted to their tongue, is to my taste a grave error. The match with certain Hauts-Médocs is far superior.

WHITE?

Thierry Nicolas has made me try a Camembert with a golden Côtes-du-Jura made by a M. Rolet. It was dazzling. Try a Gruyère from Fribourg with this same wine: the two cheeses have much the same sensory profile, and these combinations will bring you much pleasure. You can also try, with Camembert, a few slices of apple or an apple compote made with

Calvados. This latter you had better pick out from your grand-
father's cellar so that its youthful vivacity will have mellowed.
Try the same thing with a Livarot cheese. But with a Pont-
l'Evêque cheese, a good Meursault—what a joy! Alike in texture, a union of aroma, with lingering flavor—there is perfect
accord. There are other harmonies to be discovered, for example, a white Saint-Joseph with its lovely amber hue, hinting
at spice, say, from 1982. But why is it that toasted bread tastes
wrong with the Saint-Joseph? Our little game is full of surprises,
it seems, and what will work one day may be less of a success
another day, or just the reverse.

There are some combinations that are obvious and easy,
such as Crotin de Chavignol cheese with Sancerre, Charolais
cheese with a white Mâcon, Chaource cheese with a Chablis
—where the wine's liveliness envelops the fatty character of
the cheese—or a Chèvre de Valençay with a Reuilly. But do
not neglect, in this category, fresh *chèvres* from the Loire with
a dry Vouvray. L'Epoisses, a cheese with a great deal of character, cannot be served with a light wine. It demands an equal:
a *marc* de Bourgogne (but make sure that it's a good one!), but
at its very best accompany it with a Chorey-lès-Beaune . . .
Your guests will be amazed by such a display of power and
finesse: it is an olfactory combination that will fill a mouth
with fire.

Taste a Fourme d'Ambert with a Banyuls, Roquefort with a
Sauternes, and don't forget the classic pairing of Stilton and
Port, or—to change locales—Munster and Gewürztraminer or
Bleu d'Auvergne with an old Rivesaltes. The opposition between the acid and the sweet make for a combination that has
a remarkable freshness. But, above all, realize that all this is far
from definitive.

Finally, when you have time, try a sheep's-milk cheese from
Bigorre with sherry, or a Saint-Marcellin with a wine from the
Jura, a Muscat de Beaumes-de-Venise or a Jurançon.

VINE

AND SEA

◆ ◆ ◆

*It would seem that the produce of the sea
is easily paired with wine.
Yet perhaps it is exactly in this realm
that perfect harmony is difficult to discover,
as the following evidence will show.*

IZHAR COHEN

Looking for a harmonious match between food and wine often stirs up discord, since taste is a very lively and arbitrary sense, unstable and changeable, much like fashion.

Thus fish soups or *bouillabaisse* obviously call for Provençal whites, such as Cassis or Château-Simone-Blanc, but I've been astonished by a Riesling and even more by sherry, that is, as long as a little of the wine was added to the soup. These issues become complex to an exaggerated degree when it comes to oysters, the qualities and origins of which are infinite. The compatibility between *creuse* oysters from Brittany and Muscadet is obvious. But the combination of *belon* oysters and an Apremont from Savoy or *marenne* oysters and a dry Vouvray? What marvelous surprises! White Graves do not make for a felicitous match, it seems, except with cultivated oysters, a little on the fatty side. While oysters *à la bordelaise* (served with little sausages or croutons lightly spread with foie gras) may enchant when served with a chilled young red Graves, the same oysters will elicit a grimace if served with a watercress sauce and the identical wine! *Bouzigue* oysters from the Mediterranean, which are notable for their particular iodine taste, will smile at a young

bottle of red from the Côtes du Roussillon—that is evident—
but a red Graves will get the cold shoulder.

OYSTERS AND RIESLING

Yet how is it that all these briny ladies, each with her individual
personality, are so fond of Riesling, that king of the Alsatian
varietals? And why is it that *creuse* oysters from Brittany are
appreciative of red Sancerre and oysters from the North Sea
prefer to amuse themselves with a Sylvaner?

And on the subject of another combination, Champagne and
caviar: I am of the opinion that they usually don't go together.
These two luxury foods usually come to blows, that is, unless
you can serve a Bollinger RD or another very vinous Champagne. If you don't like vodka, consider a Tokay from Alsace,
also known as Pinot Gris. But above all, don't forget the whole
wheat bread or, even better, the sublime potato, the prettiest
match caviar will ever know.

A WIDE SELECTION
FOR CRUSTACEANS

For crustaceans that will be served cold with mayonnaise, the
choice is relatively simple. Numerous varietals will do nicely,
beginning with Riesling, Chardonnay, and also Sauvignon
Blanc (only a Graves) without forgetting Pinot Blanc from
either Alsace or Burgundy. However, if the sauce is spicy or
scented with herbs, consider a wine made of the Roussanne
grape combined with the Vigonier from the Rhône Valley or
phe same varietal mixed with the Savagnin from the Jura. Lobster, that master of the sea, could be allied only with its equal,
Corton-Charlemagne or Montrachet. However, my recipe for
Lobster with Vanilla will respond only to a Meursault. Other
lobster recipes that are made with red wine should be served
with the wine used in the sauce.

If a sauce contains curry and is to be served with fish, consider a Condrieu or a Tokay. While a grilled crayfish may prefer a Riesling, when served with a cream sauce it offers itself totally to a Chablis, as is often the case for other crayfish dishes. Bass with a white wine sauce is an invitation to a white Burgundy; when served with an emulsion of olive oil and fennel, however, it calls for a good white Châteauneuf-du-Pape.

UNUSUAL UNIONS

Setting aside vodka and aquavit, have you yet tried a dry Jurançon, a white Loire, or a Pouilly-sur-Loire with smoked fish? (Especially smoked salmon with the Jurançon?) These matches are a superb success. But don't let yourself be had by Pouilly "Fumé." This appellation cannot stand the taste of smoked fish, turning metallic and disagreeable. On the other hand, fresh salmon with citrus goes superbly with wines made of the Sauvignon grape.

Let's enlarge the subject of seafood to include frogs' legs and *escargots* (snails). The first, in rustic preparations, are good company for a Bourgogne Aligoté, or an Entre-Deux-Mers, but with *mousserons* (a delicate wild mushroom) they are in need of a white Pernand-Vergelesses. With a little anise or fennel, they will be pleased to bed down with a white Châteauneuf-du-Pape. The same is true for *escargots*. If they are cooked in the classic way with garlic butter, serve a Bourgogne Aligoté or a Riesling. With *cèpes*, however, they require a Cahors, a Madiran, or a Santenay.

The appellation of a wine and the ingredients of a recipe speak to us powerfully as a result of their geography and aromas. It is this ensemble which we must consult in our imagination. But don't ever forget the texture of a food. Thus monkfish, firm and white, clamors for a red wine with youthful tannin.

These examples, assuredly too brief, reveal to us mysteries that are sometimes difficult to explain. Furthermore, to be more precise, we should introduce the notion of a vintage, which gives the precise profile of a wine, since, as the poet says, "a wine is truth concealed."

ANCIENT
REMAINS

◆ ◆ ◆

Under the Ancien Régime,
the officers charged with the king's table
used to make a business out of selling
royal leftovers to restaurants and take-out shops.
Let us look into the rich repertoire
of recipes for leftovers.

◆◆◆◆◆◆◆◆◆◆◆◆◆◆◆◆◆◆◆◆◆◆◆◆◆◆◆◆◆◆◆◆◆◆◆◆◆◆◆

As a follow-up to the recipes for Pot-au-feu Salad, Croquettes, Boiled Beef Lyonnaise, à la Diable, and à la Poulette, here are five more recipes that make the most of leftover food.

LEFTOVER CHICKEN
WITH CURRY SAUCE

◆ ◆ ◆

Emincé de volaille au curry

Serves 1 to 2

1 small onion	⅔ cup heavy cream
½ apple	Salt and pepper
1 tablespoon butter	Cooked chicken
1 tablespoon curry powder or to taste	

Chop the onion, and core and dice the apple. Heat the butter in a saucepan over moderate heat, add the onion and apple and sauté until the onion is soft and transparent. Add the curry powder and cook over moderately low heat for 5 minutes. Add the cream and simmer 10 to 15 minutes longer. Season with salt and pepper. Spoon the sauce over sliced left-over roast chicken (*or turkey*) and serve with a rice pilaf.

Wine: Condrieu

LEFTOVER CHICKEN *BONNE FEMME*

◆ ◆ ◆

Emincé de volaille à la bonne femme

Slice thin leftover meat from a roast chicken (*or turkey*). Add ham, which you have cut into thin strips. There should be 4 parts chicken to 1 part ham. Combine this with an equal amount of cooked rice and cover with Béchamel sauce (see Appendix). Spoon into a baking dish, sprinkle with grated cheese and a little butter and bake in a hot oven until it is heated through. Set briefly under a broiler to brown the top.

Wine: White Côtes-du-Jura

HACHIS PARMENTIER

◆ ◆ ◆

Serves 8

2 pounds boiled beef	1 pound lean sausage meat
4 or 5 large onions	(optional)
2 pounds potatoes	Pepper
½ pound butter	1 cup chopped parsley
Salt	1 cup milk

Remove any fat or gristle from the meat. Grind in a meat grinder or food processor. Set aside. Peel and dice the onions. Peel the potatoes and set aside, covered with cold water.

Heat 3 tablespoons of the butter in a large flameproof casserole over moderate heat. Add the onions and cook, covered,
for 10 to 12 minutes. In the meantime, simmer the potatoes
in lightly salted water.

Before the onions begin to brown, add the sausage meat (if
using) and mix with the onions. Cook, stirring, for 6 to 7
minutes. Add the ground beef and season with salt and pepper.
Incorporate 7 tablespoons butter, tablespoon by tablespoon,
into this mixture. Stir in the parsley. Spread this hash in a
baking pan to a thickness of about 1½ inches.

Preheat the oven to 400° F.

Once the potatoes are cooked, drain and mash. Stir in the
milk and the remaining butter. Spread the mashed potatoes
evenly over the hash and bake for 20 to 25 minutes. Set under
the broiler to lightly brown the top. Serve hot, accompanied
by a green salad, preferably made with *frisée* or curly endive
and dressed with a vinaigrette made with sherry vinegar.

HUNGARIAN MEAT LOAF

◆ ◆ ◆

Pain de boeuf à la hongroise

Serves 4 to 6

1 pound boiled beef	Butter
¾ cup bread crumbs	Flour
2½ cups beef broth	2 medium-sized onions
½ teaspoon chopped garlic	1 shallot
1 teaspoon chopped parsley	1 cup chopped mushrooms
3 whole eggs	⅓ cup dry white wine
Salt	1 tablespoon chopped herbs
¼ teaspoon paprika	(parsley, chervil, tarragon)
3 egg whites	Pepper

Preheat the oven to 350° F.

Chop the beef coarsely and combine with the bread crumbs,

½ cup of the broth, and the garlic and parsley. Grind in a meat grinder or food processor. Be careful not to grind it too fine if you use the latter. Mix in the whole eggs and season with salt and the paprika. Beat the egg whites until stiff and carefully fold into the meat mixture. Lightly butter a charlotte mold or a loaf pan and fill with the meat mixure. Cover with buttered parchment or foil.

Set the mold in a larger pan and fill with boiling water at least two thirds of the way up the sides of the mold. Bake about 1 hour, until firm. Unmold onto a deep serving platter.

Heat 1½ tablespoons butter in a small saucepan, add 1 tablespoon flour, and cook briefly. Add the remaining 2 cups broth, bring to a boil, and simmer 15 minutes, or until it is reduced by about half.

In the meantime, chop the onions and shallot fine. Heat 2 tablespoons butter in a skillet over moderate heat. Add the onions, shallot, and mushrooms and sauté until the onions are soft and translucent. Add the white wine and boil until it is almost completely evaporated, then add the reduced broth. Let it cook until it thickens slightly. Add the herbs, remove from the heat, and gradually stir in 1½ tablespoons butter, bit by bit. Season with salt and pepper to taste. Spoon over the meat loaf.

CROUSTADES À L'ANCIENNE

◆ ◆ ◆

You can use any one of a number of meats for this recipe: leftover boiled or roast beef, chicken, or turkey works equally well.

Serves 2

2 (1-inch-thick) slices white bread	Butter or oil
Milk	1 cup chopped leftover meat
Flour	2 tablespoons *crème fraîche*
Egg yolks	4 tablespoons grated Gruyère cheese
Bread crumbs	Salt and pepper

Preheat the oven to 450° F.

Cut the crusts off the bread and hollow out the center, making a kind of bowl out of each slice. Dip them in milk, then flour, then beaten egg yolks, and finally in the bread crumbs. Heat about ½ cup butter or oil in a large skillet and fry the bread slices on both sides, until golden. Drain on paper towels.

Stir the meat with the *crème fraîche*, 2 egg yolks, and the Gruyère. Season with salt and pepper. Top the bread with this mixture and bake about 15 minutes, until golden. Serve with steamed spinach, spinach puree, or a green salad.

◆◆◆◆◆◆◆◆◆◆◆◆◆◆◆◆◆◆◆◆◆◆◆◆◆◆◆◆◆◆◆◆◆◆◆◆◆

IN HONOR
OF SAINTS

◆ ◆ ◆

*Myths and traditions—as the calendar turns,
saints' days also remind us of the history of cuisine.
With* saint-pierre *and* saint-florentin, *gourmandise
encounters legend.*

S t. Michael's Day, September 29, is a holiday dedicated
to pastry chefs. Why this particular choice? A mystery. Could
it be a kind of irony? Saint Michael was charged with crushing
the revolt of the evil angels and casting them out of paradise,
along with the sin of gourmandise . . . That Saint Bartholomew
is invoked as a patron saint of butchers is more understandable,
since he was flayed alive. When it comes to Saint Lawrence
(August 10), he certainly deserves to be the patron saint of
cooks, caterers, and restaurateurs. Apparently, this martyr
mocked his executioner: "Saint Sixtus II, the Pope from 257 to
258, was decapitated in the middle of a clandestine ceremony
he was celebrating in a cemetery on the Appian Way. Six of
the seven deacons who surrounded him were executed at the
same time. The only one who was temporarily reprieved was
deacon Lawrence, the Pope's treasurer, on the condition that
he deliver all the Church's treasures in four days. When the
time had elapsed, Saint Lawrence returned, followed by a band
of paupers and cripples. 'Here, take them, our riches,' he said,
presenting them to the imperial magistrate. 'Tell the emperor
to take good care of them, since we will no longer be there

to watch over them.' He was then laid down on a hot grill, over a slow flame, until he died. But, through the grace of God, Lawrence did not feel a thing. At the right moment, he said to his executioner, 'My back is cooked; turn me over if you want the emperor to have his meat cooked well enough to eat.' And he died praying for the Eternal City."

Saint-pierre (John Dory) is also called *zée*—well known to French players of Scrabble. This rock fish—one of the most delicate—has a large black spot on each side of its body, which, according to legend, is the imprint of Saint Peter's fingers. The fish, caught in the nets of a fisherman by the name of Peter, lamented and cried over its fate. The fisherman, moved by its despair, picked it up delicately between two fingers and threw it back in the sea.

PAN-FRIED JOHN DORY

WITH SAGE BUTTER

◆ ◆ ◆

Saint-pierre meunière au beurre de sauge

John Dory, saint-pierre in French, is difficult to obtain in North America. However, striped bass or red snapper makes for a handsome stand-in.

Serves 4

4 large sage leaves
10 tablespoons butter
½ onion
3 medium-sized tomatoes
3 tablespoons olive oil
2 strands saffron
Salt and pepper
1 cup heavy cream
2 tablespoons chopped parsley
1 pound potatoes

½ cup milk
8 oil-cured black olives
2 John Dory, each about 2 pounds
½ teaspoon coarse salt
4 bay leaves
6 large sprigs of thyme
1 pound caul fat (*see note, page 122*)
2 thin slices of white bread
1 teaspoon lemon juice

Chop the sage leaves. Melt 8 tablespoons of the butter, add the sage, and set aside at least 30 minutes.

Chop the ½ onion. Peel, seed, and quarter the tomatoes. Heat 1 tablespoon of the olive oil in a skillet over moderate heat, add the onion, and sauté until soft. Add the tomatoes and saffron and cook about 45 minutes over moderately low heat. Puree in a food processor or press through a coarse sieve. The mixture should be quite thick. Season with salt and pepper. Keep warm.

Pour the cream into a non-reactive saucepan. Boil to reduce by one half. Add the parsley and simmer for 5 minutes. Season with salt and pepper. Keep warm.

Preheat the oven to 350° F.

Peel the potatoes and simmer in lightly salted water. Once the potatoes are soft, drain and mash. Stir in the milk. Pit and chop the olives and mix into the potatoes along with the remaining 2 tablespoons olive oil. Season with salt and pepper.

Sprinkle the fish with the coarse salt and place the bay leaves and thyme sprigs on them. Wrap with a single layer of the caul fat. Bake for 12 to 15 minutes, turning halfway through.

Using a cookie cutter, cut 8 (1½-inch) rounds out of the bread. Melt the remaining butter and fry the croutons until golden.

When the fish is cooked, remove it from the oven and let rest for a few minutes. Remove the caul fat and gently fillet the fish.

To serve, place 2 scoops of the mashed potato on each plate. On each side position a crouton; top one with the tomato puree and the other with the parsley cream. Reheat the sage butter and season with salt and pepper and the lemon juice. Place a fish fillet on each plate, top with the butter, and serve immediately.

Wine: Condrieu

FLORENTINES

◆ ◆ ◆

Saint-florentin

Makes about 20

9 tablespoons *crème fraîche*
1 cup sugar
9 tablespoons honey
1 cup candied orange peel,
   diced

3½ tablespoons flour
2½ cups slivered almonds
5 ounces bittersweet
   chocolate

Combine the *crème fraîche*, sugar, honey, and orange peel in a non-reactive saucepan. Bring to a boil, stirring frequently, and boil for 5 minutes, until the mixture is lightly caramelized. Stir in the flour and almonds.

Butter 2 or more cookie sheets. Preheat the oven to 400° F.

Lay out 20 (4-inch) metal rings on the cookie sheets. Spread about 1 tablespoon of the mixture in each ring. Bake in the preheated oven for 5 to 8 minutes, until the cookies are a light golden brown.

Remove the cookie sheets from the oven and let cool briefly. Using a metal spatula, remove the warm cookies from the sheets and let cool.

Melt the chocolate and spread a thin layer on the flat side of each cookie. Allow to cool once more.

Wine: Rivesaltes

MANGO
MARVELS

◆ ◆ ◆

The mango is the sacred tree under which
the Buddha used to meditate at length.
Originating in India, its name
derives from the Tamil.
Today it has become democratized,
and we get our mangoes from India and Africa,
Peru and Egypt.

◆◆◆◆◆◆◆◆◆◆◆◆◆◆◆◆◆◆◆◆◆◆◆◆◆◆◆◆◆◆◆◆◆◆◆◆◆

The Indian mango, most notably those grown in Assam and Myammar, is a beautiful tree that can reach some 40 feet in height. Its dark green foliage is so thick that light cannot pass through, and no plant will grow in its immediate vicinity. The little village of Burail, in the Punjab, took pride in having the largest-known mango tree. It was seventy feet tall and thirty-three feet in circumference and had a harvest of five tons of fruit each year! The weight of the fruit can vary from 2 ounces to 6½ pounds. In their wild state, mangoes sometimes give off a strong turpentine smell, but when they are grafted and selected, their flesh becomes fragrant. An attempt is often made to compare their taste to that of other fruits, such as peaches, apricots, and melons. But there is no comparison that will convey their exceptional and specific flavor. Mangoes were long unknown in Europe, where they were introduced only in the twentieth century. After bananas and citrus fruits, mangoes are the most widely eaten fruit in the world. Since 1950, Europe has been importing several thousand tons per year.

Mangoes, for each 3½-ounce serving, contain about 62 calories. They are among the fruits richest in vitamin A and

contain as much vitamin C as an orange, as well as B vitamins
and plenty of iron. When ripe, they are a stimulant, diuretic,
and laxative, recommended for rheumatism and to those prone
to vascular disease. In Asia and in the Caribbean, mangoes are
used while still green, both raw and cooked, in hors d'oeuvre
or as an accompaniment to fish or meat. In Nepal, the fruit is
energetically kneaded, the skin pierced, and the juice drunk
directly. Some add it to coconut milk. In India, mangoes, along
with eggplant, are served with river fish. You can make them
into jelly, jam, or sorbet, but it is mango chutney that has a
reputation. Once ripe, mangoes will not last long. Mangoes
are eaten like an avocado, with a small spoon, with a few drops
of lemon juice, or as is. You can also serve them cut into thick
slices, unpeeled, or cut the pulp into dice, especially if you are
going to add it to a composed salad.

MANGO RELISH

◆ ◆ ◆

Rougail de mangues

*Ideally, the chili pepper called for in this recipe should be the small incendiary
pepper known variously as the* habanero *(in Mexico),* Scotch bonnet *(in
the British Caribbean), and* piment oiseu *(in the French Caribbean). It
is widely available in markets catering to a Caribbean population.*

Serves 4 to 5

3 medium-sized mangoes	1 small chili pepper
½ onion or ½ bunch of scallions	3 tablespoons vegetable oil
	Salt and pepper

Peel the mangoes and pass the pulp through a food mill,
along with the chopped onion or chopped scallions. Chop the
chili, combine with the mango mixture, oil, and salt and pepper

and pound all this in a mortar or process in a food processor.

Refrigerate 1 hour before serving. This condiment from Guadeloupe can also be served as an hors d'oeuvre.

ROAST DUCK WITH MANGO

♦ ♦ ♦

Canard aux mangues

Chef Senderens calls for 3-pound ducks, which you will have a hard time finding since the average Long Island duck is about 4½ pounds. You can either substitute a Muscovy duck or increase the cooking time by about half. See the note page 146, concerning doneness.

Serves 4

2 onions
1 carrot
2 ducks, each about 3
  pounds
Salt and pepper
2 medium-sized mangoes (a
  little underripe)

1 lemon
3 tablespoons butter
2 tablespoons minced fresh
  ginger or ½ teaspoon
  cinnamon

Preheat the oven to 425° F.

Cut the onions and carrot into large dice and strew on a roasting pan. Prick the ducks all over with a fork and rub with a little salt and pepper. Set in the oven and roast for 5 minutes per pound. Halfway through the cooking, add a tablespoon of water to the pan.

In the meantime, peel the mangoes, cut them off the pit, but leave in large pieces. Using a vegetable peeler, remove 2 (½-inch-by-2-inch) strips of lemon rind. Combine the mangoes, butter, lemon rind, and ginger or cinnamon in a small saucepan. Cover and simmer over low heat for 15 minutes.

The duck is done when the breast is still pink. Set the ducks on a serving platter and keep warm. Pour off as much fat as possible from the roasting pan while retaining any juices. Add the mangoes to the roasting pan, allowing them to soak in the juices. Arrange the mangoes on the serving platter around the ducks. Add 1 cup water to the roasting pan, set over moderately high heat, bring to a boil, and scrape the bottom of the pan to dissolve any brown bits. Reduce to ½ cup. Strain. Serve the ducks with the mangoes and the pan juices.

Wine: Condrieu

CHICKEN WITH MANGO
AND COCONUT MILK

◆ ◆ ◆

Poulet sauté aux mangues et au lait de coco

Serves 4

3½-to-4-pound chicken	1 tablespoon chopped fresh
Salt and pepper	ginger
1 onion	6 tablespoons coconut milk
1 tablespoon vegetable oil	(*see note, page 270*)
1 tablespoon butter	¼ teaspoon Cayenne pepper
2 ripe mangoes	

Cut the chicken into 8 pieces and sprinkle with salt and pepper. Chop the onion. Heat the oil and butter in a flameproof casserole over moderate heat. Add the onion and sauté until soft and translucent. Add the thigh and leg pieces, cover, and cook for 5 minutes. Add the remaining chicken. Peel the mangoes, remove the pits, cut into good-sized pieces, and add to the casserole along with the ginger. Continue cooking, covered, for 5 more minutes. Add the coconut milk and cook until the meat is cooked through, an additional 15 to 20 minutes. Season with the Cayenne. Taste and adjust the seasoning. Serve with rice.

Wine: Condrieu, white Châteauneuf-du-Pape

MANGO SALAD WITH

PASSION FRUIT AND RUM

◆ ◆ ◆

Salade de mangues aux fruits de la Passion et au rhum

Serves 4

3 ripe mangoes
3 tablespoons rum (*see
page 272*)

3 passion fruit

Peel and slice the mangoes. Arrange the slices on individual plates; sprinkle with the rum. Scoop out the passion fruit pulp and spoon it over the slices. Refrigerate for 30 minutes before serving.

Serve with white rum.

MANGO SORBET

◆ ◆ ◆

Sorbet de mangues

Serves 4 to 6

4 large ripe mangoes
1 cup sugar

Juice of 1 lemon

Peel the mangoes and remove the pits. Puree the pulp in a blender or food processor. Measure 2 cups. Refrigerate.

Combine the sugar with 2 cups water. Bring to a boil until the sugar is completely dissolved. Chill. Combine with the mango puree and the lemon juice. Freeze in an ice cream maker, following the manufacturer's directions.

Serve with a garnish of fresh raspberries.

Wine: Muscat de Rivesaltes

COOKING
WITH A PLUM

◆ ◆ ◆

The green of the greengage plum,
the yellow of the mirabelle,
the purple of the Italian plum:
a palate for a cook's designs.
In tarts, clafoutis, and jam,
but also as a garnish for meat or poultry.

◆◆◆◆◆◆◆◆◆◆◆◆◆◆◆◆◆◆◆◆◆◆◆◆◆◆◆◆◆◆◆◆◆◆◆◆◆◆◆

Plums have been cultivated in Syria since ancient times. It was at Damascus that the Crusaders' advance was halted in 1148. While they could not storm the city, they did bring back its fruit, which is how we get the expression *y aller pour des prunes* (literally "to go there for the plums"), meaning to go for bagatelles. We know from Pliny that there were already numerous varieties of plums in Italy in his time, and that the most ancient of these was the Damascus plum. It seems that the Romans were the first to graft plum trees; thus, over the centuries, the varieties have multiplied.

We may each have our favorite plum, but isn't the *reine-claude* (the greengage) queen of them all? It dates from the (short) reign of Claude of France, daughter to Louis XII and wife to François I, "the flower and pearl among the women of her time, a mirror of goodness, without a single blemish, who was grievously lamented." Following in this royal line, we have the *prune de Monsieur*, honoring the brother of Louis XIV. In 1750, we find the *galissonnière*, imported by Roland Michel Barrin, Marquis de La Galissonnière, on his return from a voyage to Canada, where he had traveled to determine the borders of the French possessions.

DUCK BREASTS WITH PLUMS

◆ ◆ ◆

Canard aux prunes

The duck breasts should ideally be taken from the moulard duck, *the same bird used for producing foie gras; however, any boneless duck breast will do.*

Serves 4

2 pounds very sweet plums	Salt and pepper
2 cups dry red wine	4 boneless duck breasts
¼ bouillon cube	7 tablespoons butter
¼ teaspoon cinnamon	Coarsely ground white
¼ teaspoon five-spice	pepper
powder (*see note, page 101*)	

Pit the plums and combine in a large non-reactive saucepan with the wine, bouillon cube, cinnamon, half the five-spice powder, and a little salt and pepper. Bring to a boil and then cook at a bare simmer for about 15 minutes. When the fruit begins to fall apart, gently strain it, reserving the juices.

With a sharp knife, score the skin side of the duck breasts at ½-inch intervals almost down to the flesh. Heat a large skillet over moderate heat and add the breasts, skin side down; cook for about 10 minutes, until the skin is very crisp. Turn over and cook for about 4 minutes longer. Allow to rest for 10 minutes in a warm place.

Boil the plum juices in a wide saucepan until the liquid becomes syrupy. Over very low heat, gradually stir in the butter, a small piece at a time. Season with salt, pepper, and the remaining five-spice powder.

Slice the breasts, arrange on individual plates, and spoon the sauce around them. Sprinkle with the coarsely ground white pepper. Garnish with a spoonful of the drained plums. You could accompany the dish with scoops of spinach puree.

Serve with a Cahors (vintages 1979 through 1982). With its beautiful brilliant color, its subtle scents where ripe fruit dominates, all finesse and distinction, with its roundness and fullness in the mouth, this wine is the ideal companion for duck with plums.

PLUM *CLAFOUTIS*

◆ ◆ ◆

Clafoutis aux prunes

Serves 4 to 6

2 cups milk
¾ pound brioche, challah, or other enriched egg bread
10 tablespoons softened butter
3 eggs

1 cup sugar
1 teaspoon vanilla
¼ teaspoon *quatre-épices (see note, page 54)*
1 pinch nutmeg
2¼ pounds plums

Preheat the oven to 350° F.

Boil the milk. Crumble the brioche and set aside. Combine the butter, eggs, and sugar and beat until light and fluffy. Add the vanilla, *quatre-épices*, and nutmeg. Pit the plums.

Stir the hot milk into the butter mixture, add the plums and brioche, and mix well. Spoon into a buttered mold. Bake for 45 minutes.

Serve with a plum *eau-de-vie* such as *vielle prune* from Agen or Souillac.

THREE-PLUM TART

◆ ◆ ◆

Tartes aux trois prunes

Chef Senderens calls for three types of plums: purple Italian plums, mirabelles, which are very small, yellow, and perfumed; and greengage plums, which are a little larger and yellowish green. Should the latter two be difficult to obtain, substitute another two varieties.

Serves 6

30 Italian plums	9 greengage plums
Zest of 2 oranges	2 cups confectioners' sugar
7 tablespoons granulated sugar	1 teaspoon cinnamon
18 *mirabelles*	1 recipe Pastry Dough (*see Appendix*)

Take 18 of the Italian plums, cut in half, and remove the pits. Combine in a non-reactive saucepan with the orange zest and granulated sugar. Cover and cook over low heat, until the plums fall apart.

Preheat the oven to 400° F.

Cut all the remaining plums in half and remove the pits. Arrange each variety in a separate baking dish, combine the confectioners' sugar and cinnamon, and dust all the plums with this mixture. Bake for about 15 minutes for the larger plums and 8 minutes for the smaller *mirabelles*.

In the meantime, roll out the dough about ⅛ inch thick. Cut out 6 (6-inch) circles and arrange on a cookie sheet. Prick all over with a fork. Set the oven at 375° F. and bake until golden, about 10 to 15 minutes.

Spread each warm base with the cooked plum compote and top with the baked plum halves: a ring of the Italian plums on the outside, the greengages inside this ring, and finally the *mirabelles* in the center. Serve warm, accompanied by a scoop of vanilla ice cream, if you wish.

Serve with an *eau-de-vie*, such as *prune*, Quetsch, or Mirabelle.

◆◆◆◆◆◆◆◆◆◆◆◆◆◆◆◆◆◆◆◆◆◆◆◆◆◆◆◆◆◆◆◆◆◆◆◆

PEARLS TO
CULTIVATE

◆ ◆ ◆

*Black currants, those delicious berries
which give us exquisite liqueur and jam,
were at one time used for traditional healing.
Today, they contribute their succulent taste
to baking as well as cooking.*

◆◆◆◆◆◆◆◆◆◆◆◆◆◆◆◆◆◆◆◆◆◆◆◆◆◆◆◆◆◆◆◆◆◆◆◆◆◆

With the aid of black currants, every venom that comes from "fruit infected by toad's breath" may be neutralized, "tertian ague, quartan fever, plague, and pox can be cured, and worms chased out of small children and adults. It is the quickest remedy for reviving an apoplectic, for rousing from a lethargic slumber, for combating the vapors in women. It purges, cheers, fortifies the brain, prevents colds, dispels migraines, heals wounds, cures jaundice, cleanses the spleen and liver, loosens sand and gravel, tempers the fire of bile, breaks down the aggravating vapors of melancholy." This was the Abbé Bailly de Montaran writing in 1712, thus turning black currants into a panacea and making them famous.

Black currants originate in Europe. They grow wild in France, in the forests and valleys of the Auvergne, in Piedmont, in Switzerland, in Sweden, as well as in Siberia. They were already being grown for the table in 1571, but their cultivation really got under way in France, in the Côte-d'Or, only when the celebrated liqueur Cassis of Dijon was perfected. The smaller variety of black currants is exceptionally aromatic and flavorful. The fruit with the larger berries is less concentrated and more watery. Black currants are rich in Vitamin C, potassium, and calcium.

LAMB BRAINS WITH

BLACK CURRANT BUTTER

◆ ◆ ◆

Cervelle au beurre de cassis

Serves 4

8 lamb brains	¾ cup black currant juice
Vinegar	¾ cup plus 2 tablespoons
2 sprigs of thyme	butter
2 bay leaves	½ cup black currants
Salt and pepper	12 leaves Italian parsley
12 baby carrots	

Prepare the lamb brains by soaking them in lightly vinegared water for 1 hour in the refrigerator. Remove the membrane that covers them. Combine the thyme and bay leaves with 4 cups water, season with salt and pepper. Bring to a boil, add the brains, and simmer for 5 minutes. Drain and cool under cold running water.

Clean the carrots, leaving a small piece of the stem attached. Cook in lightly salted water for 5 to 6 minutes.

Boil the currant juice in a non-reactive saucepan until it is syrupy and thick. Set over very low heat and gradually stir in the ¾ cup butter, small piece by small piece, until it is all incorporated and you have an unctuous sauce. Remove from the heat.

Season the brains with salt and pepper. Heat the remaining 2 tablespoons butter in a large skillet over moderately high heat. When the butter is sizzling, add the brains, and brown on all sides.

To serve, spoon the sauce onto plates or a serving platter. Arrange the brains on top and scatter the carrots, black currants, and parsley leaves on the sauce. Serve immediately.

Wine: Saint-Aubin or red Savigny-lès-Beaune

DUCK BREASTS WITH

BLACK CURRANTS

◆ ◆ ◆

Filets de canard aux baies de cassis

Serves 4

4 duck breasts	⅔ cup bottled black currants
Salt and pepper	(preferably unsweetened)
⅔ cup black currant juice	Coarsely ground white
1½ cups chicken broth	pepper
3 tablespoons butter	

Preheat the oven to 450° F.

With a sharp knife, score the skin side of the duck breasts at ½-inch intervals almost down to the flesh. Season with salt and pepper to taste. Heat a large skillet over moderately high heat, add the breasts, skin side down, and cook for about 10 minutes, until the skin is crisp. Put the breasts in the oven, skin side up, and continue cooking for about 10 more minutes. The breasts should still be rare inside.

In the meantime, pour the black currant juice into a wide saucepan over high heat. Boil to reduce by half. Add the chicken broth and continue boiling until you have only ⅔ cup liquid left. Remove from the heat and stir in the butter, adding a small piece at a time. Drain the black currants and add to the sauce.

To serve, slice the breasts, arrange on plates, and cover with the sauce. Sprinkle with the coarsely ground white pepper.

Wine: Aloxe-Corton or Chambolle-Musigny

BLACK CURRANT TART

◆ ◆ ◆

Tarte au cassis

Serves 8

PÂTE SABLÉE

1¾ cups flour
½ cup confectioners' sugar
2 vanilla beans

13 tablespoons butter
6–8 tablespoons heavy cream

1¼ cups granulated sugar
1¾ pounds black currants

5 mint leaves

Make the *pâte sablée*. Sift together the flour and confectioners' sugar. Split the vanilla beans, scrape out the centers, and add to the flour. Using your hands or a pastry cutter, break up the butter in the flour until the mixture is about as fine as rolled oats. Alternatively, pulse in a food processor until this texture is achieved. Add enough cream so that the mixture just sticks together. Wrap in plastic wrap and refrigerate at least 1 hour.

Preheat the oven to 350° F.

Roll the dough out ⅛ inch thick and line a 10-inch tart pan with it. Prick all over with a fork and bake for 20 to 30 minutes, until golden.

Combine the granulated sugar with ⅔ cup water in a saucepan. Bring to a boil, add the black currants, and cook at a bare simmer for 15 minutes. When the crust is cooked, drain the currants and use them to fill the tart shell. Chop the mint leaves and sprinkle on top. Cool to room temperature. It is best to prepare the tart several hours before you plan on serving it.

Serve with *crème de cassis*.

BLACK CURRANT SORBET

◆ ◆ ◆

Sorbet au cassis

Serves 4 to 6

1 cup sugar
4 cups black currant juice

Juice of 1 lemon

Combine the sugar with a cup of water in a saucepan, bring to a boil, then chill. Combine with the black currant and lemon juices. Freeze in an ice cream maker, following the manufacturer's directions. Serve while still a little soft.

◆◆◆◆◆◆◆◆◆◆◆◆◆◆◆◆◆◆◆◆◆◆◆◆◆◆◆◆◆◆◆◆◆◆◆◆◆◆◆

APPENDIX:

BASIC RECIPES

TO PEEL TOMATOES

◆ ◆ ◆

Core the tomatoes and cut a small X in the bottom of each. Plunge them into boiling water to cover for 20 to 30 seconds, then cool under cold water. Peel.

MAYONNAISE

◆ ◆ ◆

Makes 2 cups

2 egg yolks
2 tablespoons lemon juice
   (or more)

1 tablespoon Dijon mustard
1½ cups oil*
Salt and pepper

Stir together the egg yolks, 2 tablespoons lemon juice, and the mustard. Drop by drop, whisk in the oil until it is fully

* Use vegetable or olive oil or a combination of the two; olive oil will make a heavier mayonnaise.

incorporated. Season with salt and pepper and with more lemon juice if you like.

PASTRY DOUGH

◆ ◆ ◆

Pâte brisée

Makes about ¾ pound dough

2⅓ cups all-purpose flour
1 tablespoon sugar
½ teaspoon salt

14 tablespoons unsalted butter
About ⅓ cup ice water

Sift together the flour, sugar, and salt. Cut the butter into small pieces and add to the flour. Using your hands or a pastry cutter, break up the butter in the flour until the mixture is about as fine as rolled oats.

Add just enough ice water to moisten the flour. Toss to form a rather dry dough. Do not overmix. Gather the dough together and wrap in plastic film. Refrigerate at least 2 hours.

BÉCHAMEL SAUCE

Makes 2 cups

2 cups milk
1 small onion
1 small bay leaf
1 clove

1 sprig thyme
3 tablespoons butter
6 tablespoons flour
Salt and white pepper

Combine the milk, onion, bay leaf, clove, and thyme in a non-reactive saucepan over moderate heat. Bring to a boil and simmer for 15 minutes. Strain and cool briefly.

Melt the butter in a saucepan over moderate heat. Add the

flour and cook, stirring, for 2 minutes. Add the milk, stirring vigorously. Cook at a very low simmer for 20 minutes, stirring occasionally. Strain; season to taste.

BÉARNAISE SAUCE

◆ ◆ ◆

Makes about 1 cup

¾ cup butter	¼ cup white wine
1 shallot, chopped	2 egg yolks
2 tarragon sprigs, chopped	Salt
1 teaspoon crushed	2 tablespoons chopped
peppercorns	chervil
¼ cup white wine vinegar	

Melt the butter over low heat; it should be only just melted.

Combine the shallot, tarragon, pepper, vinegar, and wine in a non-reactive saucepan and simmer until reduced to 3 tablespoons.

Strain and combine with the egg yolks in a metal bowl and whisk over very low heat or in a double boiler until light and slightly thickened. Remove from the heat and whisk in the melted butter, a little at a time. Ideally, the butter and egg yolks should be the same temperature. Add salt to taste. Stir in the chervil. The sauce can be kept warm for up to 30 minutes by setting the bowl over hot (not boiling!) water.

BEURRE BLANC

◆ ◆ ◆

Makes 1 cup

¼ cup white wine vinegar	1 cup butter
¼ cup dry white wine	Salt and white pepper
2 shallots, chopped	

Combine the vinegar, wine, and shallots in a small non-reactive saucepan over high heat. Boil to reduce to about 2 tablespoons. Set over very low heat.

Cut the butter into small pieces. Add about a quarter of the butter and stir. Continuing to stir, add the remaining butter, a piece at a time, until almost all of the butter has liquefied. When almost all of the butter has dissolved, remove from the heat. Add salt and pepper to taste. Strain. Serve immediately.

VINAIGRETTE

◆ ◆ ◆

Makes 1 cup

1 tablespoon Dijon mustard	⅔–1 cup olive oil
⅓ cup wine vinegar	Salt and pepper

Whisk together the mustard and vinegar in a small bowl. Continuing to beat the mixture, add the oil in a slow stream. Stir in salt and pepper to taste.

MAÎTRE D'HÔTEL BUTTER

◆ ◆ ◆

Serves 6

½ cup butter, softened	1 tablespoon lemon juice
2 tablespoons chopped parsley	Salt and pepper

Stir together the butter, parsley, and lemon juice and season with salt and pepper.

Serve with grilled fish and meats.

PASTA DOUGH ✳

◆ ◆ ◆

Makes 1¼ pounds dough

4 large eggs	2¾ cups all-purpose flour
1 tablespoon olive oil	Large pinch of salt

FOOD PROCESSOR METHOD:

Combine all the ingredients in the bowl of a food processor. Process 2 to 3 minutes, until the dough comes together into a ball.

Gather up the dough and knead briefly.

HAND METHOD:

Lightly beat the eggs and oil together.

Place the flour and salt in a large bowl and make a well in the center. Pour in the egg-oil mixture. Slowly mix in the flour until it is completely combined. You may need to add a few drops of water. Knead well.

Cover the dough with plastic wrap and allow to rest 10 minutes.

Cut the dough in 2, lightly flouring each piece.

Working with each piece individually, pass through the widest opening of your pasta machine. Fold in 2 and pass through again. Repeat the folding and rolling process twice more.

Reduce the thickness of the sheet gradually by adjusting the regulating knob until you reach the narrowest setting.

To make filled pasta, proceed immediately. To make cut pasta, allow the sheet to dry out for 10 minutes before cutting.

A GLOSSARY

OF WINES

AND SPIRITS

Aloxe-Corton. A village in the northern part of the Côte de Beaune region of Burgundy that produces complex red and white wines. The reds are best when well aged.

Arbois (white). Dry fruity wines from the Jura region in eastern France, based on the Chardonnay or the Savagnin grape or a combination of the two.

Bandol. At their best, splendid Provençal wines with an herbaceous perfume at times reminiscent of violets (see p. 105).

Banyuls. Fortified sweet red wines made in southwestern France, primarily from the Grenache grape. Their flavor is somewhat like that of Port.

Beaujolais. Traditionally, light and simple fruity red wines, made to be enjoyed by the carafe as soon as they were released. This is still true of Beaujolais nouveau; however, many vineyards are now making more elaborate wines.

Beaune. Classic red Burgundy of middle rank.

Bordeaux. One of France's most important wine-growing regions, making some of the best wines in the world. Most red Bordeaux are based on the Cabernet Sauvignon grape, and most whites on Sauvignon Blanc.

Burgundy. The wine region in eastern France that makes arguably the best wine in the world, with prices to match. The reds are made with the Pinot Noir grape, the whites with Chardonnay.

Calvados. A spirit distilled from apples and often aged in brandy casks.

Cassis. An austere and bone-dry white wine from Provence, with a delicate bouquet. Not to be confused with crème de cassis (see below).

Chablis. An elegant white wine of very high quality from northern Burgundy, based on the Chardonnay grape. Not to be confused with the so-called Chablis jug wines produced in California and elsewhere.

Chambolle-Musigny. Rich yet subtle red wines made in Burgundy. They reach maturity relatively early.

Champagne. Wine-growing area to the north of Paris producing world-famous sparklers.

Château-Chalon. A strong white wine (known as *vin jaune* because of its yellow color) made entirely from the Savagnin grape in the Jura region. Often served as an aperitif.

Château de Beaucastel. A recommended producer of white Châteauneuf-du-Pape (see below).

Château de Fonsalette. A recommended red Côtes-du-Rhône (see below).

Château-Grillet. A rare white wine made of the Viognier from the Côtes-du-Rhône. Similar to Condrieu (see below).

Château Lynch-Bages. A fine robust red from the Pauillac region of Bordeaux.

Châteauneuf-du-Pape (red). Very full-bodied wines, often of great character, with a bouquet evoking anise and other spices. A minimum of thirteen grape varieties are used to make the wine.

Châteauneuf-du-Pape (white). A wine possessing complex, flowery perfume with just a hint of sweetness, from the famed estate of the popes of Avignon in the South of France (see page 275).

Chignin. A light and fresh white wine made from the Jacquère grape in Savoie near the Swiss border. May be difficult to find in the United States.

Chinon. A velvety red from the Loire based on the Cabernet Franc grape. It can be light or quite unctuous, with penetrating berry flavors.

Condrieu. A rich white wine from the Côtes-du-Rhône with a subtle bouquet hinting at violets and apricot.

Coteaux-d'Aix-en-Provence. A large area producing a wide range of wines of varied quality. The whites tend to be light and fresh, the reds robust.

Coteaux-des-Baux-de-Provence. Much the same as the above.

Coteaux-du-Languedoc. A large area of southwestern France where the whites, reds, and rosés tend to be uncomplicated and fruity. Occasionally the reds will have more character.

Côte-Rôtie. A fine red from the Côtes-du-Rhône, made primarily from the Syrah grape. Long-lived and full-bodied, with a spicy perfume.

Côtes-de-Provence (white). Light wines from the South of France which, at their best, have a pleasing floral bouquet.

Côtes-du-Jura (white). Similar to Arbois (see above).

Côtes-du-Rhône. An appellation that stretches south of Burgundy in the vicinity of the Rhône River, making extremely sophisticated wines (such as Châteauneuf-du-Pape and Hermitage, both red and white) as well as very straightforward light red and white wines sold simply as Côtes-du-Rhône. The grapes used vary depending on the area.

Crème de cassis. A liqueur made with black currants in the area around Dijon.

Crozes-Hermitage. Wines made in the vineyards adjoining the famous Hermitage appellation, similar to their better-known cousins, though paler in both taste and bouquet (see Hermitage, below).

Domaine de Trévalon. A recommended Coteaux-des-Baux-de-Provence (see above).

Eau-de-vie. A clear dry spirit, usually distilled from fruit and seldom aged. Examples include Kirsch, made from cherries; Mirabelle and Quetsch, made from plums of those names; Framboise, from raspberries; and Poire William, from pears.

Fiefs Vendéens. Light, agreeable white and red wines. The whites are primarily made of Chenin Blanc and the reds of the Gamay Noir à Jus Blanc.

Gamay de Touraine. A fruity red made much like the lighter Beaujolais. Probably impossible to find in the United States.

Gevrey-Chambertin. Soft mellow Burgundies with a powerful bouquet.

Grands-Echezeaux. A rich Burgundy of much elegance and finesse. One of the greats.

Hermitage. One of the exceptional appellations in the Côtes-du-Rhône, producing opulent reds with aromas reminiscent of leather and black currants as well as elegant floral whites. The red wines are made entirely of the Syrah grape, the whites with a combination of the Roussanne and the Marsanne.

Irouleguy (red). A wine of moderate body with a taste reminiscent of dried cherries, from the French Basque country near the Spanish border (see page 109).

Jurançon. This appellation in the South, near the Pyrenees, produces both a delightful, well-balanced dessert wine and an elegant dry white with a delicate bouquet. The latter is difficult to find in the United States.

Mareuil. A recommended Fiefs Vendéens (see above).

Margaux. A Bordeaux appellation that often produces excellent rich red wine.

Maury. A powerful fortified wine with complex aromas of cooked fruit and cocoa.

Montlouis (demi-sec). A delicate and lively white wine vinified from the Chenin Blanc grape. The demi-sec will have a hint of sweetness. A sparkling Montlouis is also produced.

Morey-Saint-Denis. A red Burgundy that is rich in color, delicate in flavor, with a powerful bouquet.

Muscadet. A crisp white wine produced in the Loire.

Muscat de Rivesaltes. Fortified white wines with a powerful floral aroma.

Pauillac. An appellation in the Médoc region of Bordeaux that encompasses some of the most famous red wines in the world. The wines of Pauillac are notable for their powerful and refined bouquet and well known for their aging potential.

Pernand-Vergelesses. A light, appealing red Burgundy.

Pinot Gris. An often delicious full-bodied fruity white varietal from Alsace. Also known as Tokay d'Alsace.

Pomerol. An appellation in Bordeaux known for vigorous red wines which nevertheless exhibit much finesse.

Pommard. Rich, powerful Burgundies. They are best well aged.

Quincy. A lively dry white wine made from the Sauvignon Blanc grape in central France.

Reuilly (white). Wine similar to Quincy (above), and also from central France.

Richebourg. One of the finest vineyards in Burgundy, making powerful, perfumed (and extraordinarily expensive) wine.

Riesling. A light fruity varietal which, in France, is usually quite dry.

Rioja. One of Spain's finest wine-growing regions, making complex reds.

Saint-Aubin. Red and white Burgundies are made here, both characterized by their relative lightness.

Saint-Joseph. A vineyard in the Côtes-du-Rhône making both red and white wines. The reds are marked by a moderate body, and by aromas reminiscent of berries and spice. The relatively rare whites have a floral and honeyed perfume.

Saint-Joseph-de-Bourgueil (red). A wine made just across the river from Chinon (see above) and thus quite similar. Difficult to find in the United States.

Saint-Péray (white). A powerful dry wine from the Côtes-du-Rhône.

Sauternes. A wonderful dessert wine from Bordeaux with remarkable aging potential. When young, the wines are fruity and floral, gaining greatly in complexity as time passes.

Savigny-lès-Beaune (red). Relatively light Burgundies with a floral bouquet.

Sylvaner. A light, straightforward varietal from Alsace.

Tokay d'Alsace. See Pinot Gris.

Volnay. Elegant and supple red Burgundies from the Côte de Beaune.

Vougeot. Robust Burgundies appreciated for their rich color and powerful aroma of truffles and herbs.

Vouvray. A silky, somewhat sweet white wine made from the Chenin Blanc grape in the Loire.

INDEX